UK Price
£4.95

THE CREATIVE GARDENER'S GUIDE TO

BLUES AND PURPLES

How to mix and match over 100 stunning flowers, shrubs and trees
to create a garden of beauty

THE CREATIVE GARDENER'S GUIDE TO

BLUES AND PURPLES

How to mix and match over 100 stunning flowers, shrubs and trees
to create a garden of beauty

DAVID SQUIRE

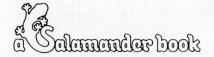

a Salamander book

Published by Salamander Books Limited
LONDON • NEW YORK

A Salamander Book

© 1986 Salamander Books Ltd.,
52 Bedford Row,
London WC1R 4LR,
United Kingdom

ISBN 0 86101 218 6

Distributed in the UK by
Hodder & Stoughton Services,
P.O. Box 6, Mill Road,
Dunton Green, Sevenoaks,
Kent TN13 2XX

All correspondence concerning the
content of this volume should be
addressed to Salamander Books Ltd.

CREDITS

AUTHOR
David Squire brings to this series practical experience both as a gardener
and holder of many horticultural awards (including the Wisley Diploma in
Horticulture and the N.K. Gould Memorial Prize from the internationally
famous Royal Horticultural Society at Wisley, Surrey) and as the author
of 14 books on gardening. He still finds time to improve and enjoy the
colourful garden at his home in West Sussex.

Editor
Jonathan Elphick

Designer
Barry Savage

Colour and monochrome reproductions
Melbourne Graphics Ltd., London, England

Filmset
Modern Text Typesetting Ltd., England

Printed in Belgium
by Proost International Book Production, Turnhout

CONTENTS

Introduction

HOW TO USE THIS BOOK

Gardeners are like painters, but with a fresh canvas available to them only once a year. Borders are planned, plant and seed catalogues avidly searched and gleaned for more vibrant and longer-lasting colours, and fellow gardeners consulted. But should you or your family have a liking for flowers of certain colours — perhaps those that contrast with established plants in your garden, blend happily against colour-washed walls, or create memories of a cherished display in a wedding bouquet — then you need further help at your elbow. You need a reliable guide which clearly portrays the range of plants within a particular part of the colour spectrum, and that is the purpose of this lavishly illustrated all-colour book.

The introductory pages explain the nature of light and colour and how different colours are measured and defined, according to their hue, value and intensity. There is also useful information on the influence of shiny or matt surfaces, why some colours are dominant and the effects of bright sunlight and the shadows of evening. Planning colour with the aid of a *colour-circle* is fully covered, and the concept of complementary and harmonizing colours is discussed in detail.

The main section of this *Creative Gardener's Guide* consists of five chapters, detailing blue and purple plants in a wide range of garden settings: filling annual and herbaceous borders, adorning rock and naturalized gardens, bringing colour to window-boxes, hanging baskets, troughs and other containers on patios and terraces, clothing bare walls, climbing trellises or serving as a harmonious framework to knit together the various elements of your garden design. Each plant is illustrated in full colour and clearly described, including its botanical and common names, height and spread (in metric and imperial units), cultivation and propagation. Within each chapter the plants are arranged alphabetically according to their botanical names. At the base of each page there are valuable tips on using combinations of plants to create colour-contrasts, subtle harmonies, focal points and interesting shapes and patterns. Flowers suitable for home decoration are also mentioned.

At the end of the book there are two comprehensive indexes. The first lists all common names, indicating if they are used in the British Isles or the United States. The second index is of botanical names, including synonyms (alternative names). The inclusion of the latter helps you identify plants botanists have recently re-classified and given new names, which are frequently sold under their old, better-known names.

This book forms part of the successful series of *Creative Gardener's Guides* and is designed to help bring further colour and interest to all gardens, whatever their size and wherever they are. Other books in this all-colour series detail the uses of *Reds and Pinks*, *Golds and Yellows*, and *Whites and Silvers*, while further gardening dimensions are revealed in the *Scented Garden* and *Variegated Garden*. Each book forms a comprehensive and concise guide to a particular range of colours or garden theme, but when formed into a colour library can benefit garden planning in a manner few other books have ever achieved.

Above: **Cercis siliquastrum**
This hardy deciduous tree is commonly known as the Judas Tree. During early summer, it bears lovely rich rose-pink flowers.

Above: **Camassia quamash**
*This dramatic purple or blue
flowered bulbous plant from
North America brings colour to
a border during mid-summer.*

Key:
1 *Cupressus glabra* 'Pyramidalis'
2 *Euonymus fortunei* 'Emerald Gold'
3 *Chamaecyparis obtusa* 'Crippsii'
4 Agapanthus
5 *Thymus* 'E. B. Anderson'

6 *Veronica prostrata* and petunias
7 *Ipomoea violacea (I. rubro-caerulea)*
8 *Hydrangea macrophylla*
9 Trailing lobelias and geraniums
10 *Clematis montana rubens*

Introduction

THE SCIENCE OF COLOUR EVALUATION

What are light and colour?

The vast range of colours we see in our gardens and homes, with their near infinite subtleties of quality, shades of light as well as intensity, can be accurately measured. But what exactly are light and colour? To state coldly and scientifically that they are forms of electromagnetic radiation clearly disregards the beauty of colour, but, technically speaking, that *is* its nature.

Electromagnetic radiation comes from the sun, and its range is wide, from gamma rays to low-frequency radio waves. But only a very small part of this extensive spectrum is in the form of visible light, from wavelengths at around 0·0004mm when the colour is deep violet, through blue, green, yellow, orange and red to deep red, when the waves are 0·0007mm. The wavelengths of purple and blue light range from 0·000492 to 0·000455mm. *See Diagram 1, below.*

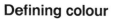

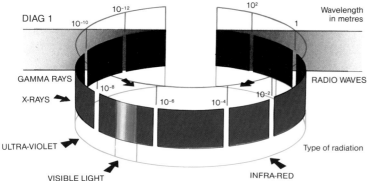

DIAG 1

Defining colour

Colours can be conceived as having three dimensions—these have been given the names *hue*, *value* and *intensity*.

Hue
This first dimension is the quality by which colours are basically distinguished one from another, such as yellow from red, green, blue or purple. For convenience, the colours so defined are those that are easily recognized, such as red, yellow, green, blue and violet. However, the Munsell System in North America defines the principal hues as red, yellow, green, blue and purple, with intermediate ones as yellow-red, green-yellow, blue-green, purple-blue and red-purple. In reality these names do no more than define points in a continuous range of hues that form a transitional and continuous band of colour. They are best conceived as a circle of pure colour, containing no white, grey or black.

If a strip of paper with ten equal divisions is marked and coloured with the five principal and five intermediate hues of the Munsell System and held in a circle the continuous range of hues and their relationship one to another can be seen.
See Diagram 2, top right.

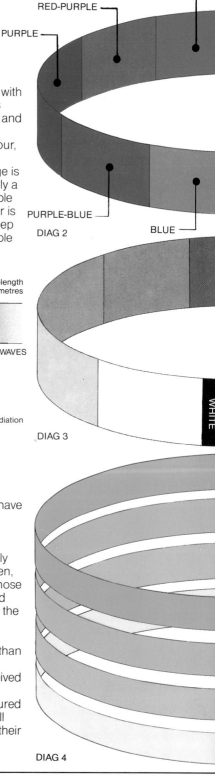

DIAG 2

DIAG 3

DIAG 4

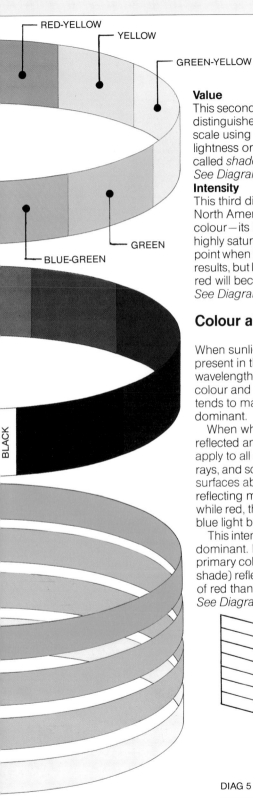

RED-YELLOW
YELLOW
GREEN-YELLOW

GREEN
BLUE-GREEN

BLACK

Value

This second dimension defines the quality by which a light colour is distinguished from a dark one. This is most easily depicted on a scale using black and white as the extremes. When defining the lightness or darkness within a colour, those with dark colours are called *shades*, while those that are light are *tints*.
See Diagram 3, centre left.

Intensity

This third dimension is also known as *saturation* or *purity*, and in North America as *chroma*. It defines the strength or weakness of a colour—its brightness or greyness. For instance, purple can be highly saturated with colour, or the pigments slowly decreased to a point when it becomes dark grey. Other colours will produce similar results, but light hues such as yellow will become light grey, whereas red will become grey.
See Diagram 4, bottom left.

Colour absorption

When sunlight falls upon coloured surfaces, a few of the colours present in the white light—which contains a mixture of all wavelengths of the visible spectrum—may be absorbed by the colour and not reflected. This is known as *colour absorption* and it tends to make primary hues, such as red, blue and yellow, more dominant.

When white light falls on a white surface, most of the rays are reflected and the subject appears white. This, however, does not apply to all surfaces. Blue surfaces absorb red, orange and yellow rays, and scatter blue, together with green, indigo and violet. Yellow surfaces absorb the blues, indigos and violets in white light, reflecting mainly yellow as well as some green, orange and red, while red, the most colour saturated of all hues, absorbs green and blue light but reflects red.

This intensification of blues, reds and yellows tends to make them dominant. Fully saturated hues reflect no more than two of the primary colours, whereas pink, which is a desaturated red (a pastel shade) reflects all three of the primary colours but a greater amount of red than of the other two colours.
See Diagram 5, below.

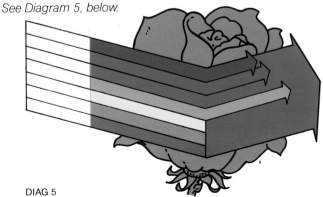

DIAG 5

Introduction

USING COLOUR IN THE GARDEN

Colour wheels

Colour wheels are frequently used to aid colour planning in the garden. When the great English scientist Sir Isaac Newton investigated light in the late 1600s, he made a wheel formed of seven colours (red, orange, yellow, green, blue, indigo and violet). During the late 1800s the American scientist A.H. Munsell researched colour assessment based on equal changes in the visual spectrum. He created a colour wheel formed of five principal colours (red, yellow, green, blue and purple, with intermediate ones between them). Other wheels have been created using four colours (red, yellow, green and blue).

However, the easiest colour circle to use is formed of three basic hues (red, yellow and blue) with three secondary ones (orange, green and violet). The secondary colours are created by overlapping the basic hues.

These colour circles indicate complementary colours (those diametrically opposite) and those that harmonize with each other (those in adjacent segments). Complementary hues are those with no common pigments, while harmonizing ones share the same pigments. Therefore, it can be seen that yellow and violet, blue and orange, red and green are complementary colours, while yellow harmonizes with green and orange, blue with green and violet, and red with orange and violet.

This colour-circle is formed by mixing coloured paints, by the process known as *subtractive colour mixing*. The other method of creating colour is by projecting three separate coloured lights (red, green and blue) onto a white surface. This process is known as *additive colour mixing* and creates colours with a different bias. *See Diagram 6, of a subtractive colour circle, below.*

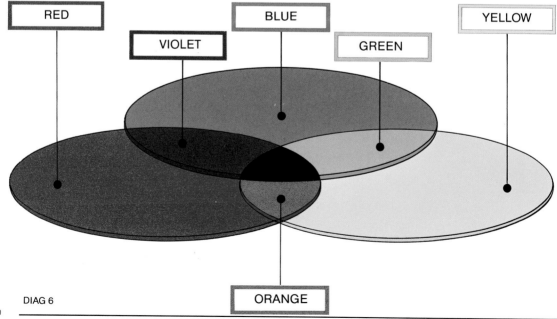

RED · VIOLET · BLUE · GREEN · YELLOW · ORANGE

DIAG 6

Shiny and matt surfaces

The surface texture of a leaf, flower or stem influences the reflected
light and its effect on the eye. A smooth surface reflects light at the
same angle at which the light hits it. This makes the light purer in
colour than the same light reflected from a matt surface. There, the
irregularities of the surface scatter the reflected light and create an
impression of dullness. Another effect of different surface texture is
that smooth surfaces appear darker and matt ones lighter. In
Nature, however, few plant surfaces are as smooth as glass, and the
scattering of reflected light occurs from most of them.
See Diagram 7, below

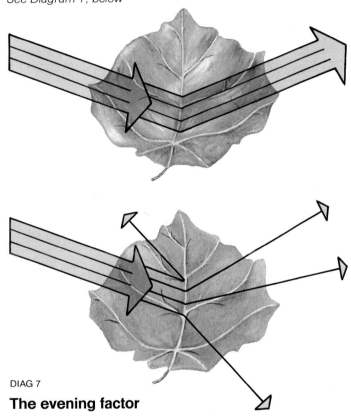

DIAG 7

The evening factor

The well-known delight of shepherds to have red sky at night,
indicating a fine tomorrow, results from a clear sky as the sun's rays
penetrate atmospheric particles and the air molecules themselves.
Even though the sky appears blue, the rays become redder,
because blue light is not created but scattered out of white light. This
change to the violet end of the spectrum makes dark colours even
darker. Blues and especially purples are made darker, while whites
and yellows are not so dramatically affected. Conversely, bright
sunshine glaring down at midday highlights light colours more than
dark ones, such as blues and purples.

Introduction

HARMONIES AND CONTRASTS IN BLUE

Ranging from delicate pure pale blues to deep purples, bright and beautiful is the key to the treasure-house of plants in this book. As a group it is rhododendrons that create much of the spring and summer blue shrub colour. The range of these shrubs is wide, from the dwarf *Rhododendron impeditum*, 15-45cm (6in-1½ft) high and with pale mauve to purple-blue flowers, through the 90cm-1·5m (3-5ft) high 'Blue Diamond', with lavender-blue flowers, to *Rhododendron augustinii*, 1·8-3m (6-10ft) high and with mauve to dark blue flowers during late spring.

There are several groups of plants whose mere mention immediately conjures up images of massed blue. These include both shrubs and herbaceous perennials. The evergreen or deciduous ceanothus shrubs from North America (chiefly California) always bring a strong burst of blue for borders or walls. And like many other plants they are often best seen in combinations. For example, *Ceanothus* x 'Cascade', with arching branches bearing small rich blue early summer flowers rises to 3m (10ft) on a wall and can be co-habited with the Mountain Clematis *Clematis montana*. Use the form 'Wilsonii' with large white flowers If the rounded evergreen Mexican Orange Blossom shrub *Choisya ternata*, with orange-scented foliage and flowers, is set in front of them they form a superb trio of scent and colour.

Delphiniums and asters are among the best known blue herbaceous plants. The tall, stately delphiniums are not easily merged into a border and are so distinctive that they are best treated as tall islands of blue spires amid other herbaceous plants. The asters, however, have such a varied height range, from *Aster alpinus* at 15cm (6in) high, with purple-blue daisy-like flowers, to the 90cm (3ft) semi-double Michaelmas Daisy *Aster novi-belgii* 'Eventide', with violet-blue flowers in late summer. Between them are several other asters, including *Aster amellus* 'Goethe' at 45-60cm (1½-2ft), with pale mauve-blue flowers.

Blue Berries and Fruits

Here is a selection of superb blue-berried plants:

Callicarpa bodinieri giraldii
Height: 1·5-1·8m (5-6ft)
A beautiful deciduous shrub with lilac-coloured flowers during late summer, followed by pale violet-purple or dark lilac berries.

Clerodendron trichotomum
Height: 3-3·5m (10-12ft)
A bushy, though sometimes open, deciduous shrub with turquoise-blue berries in autumn; for lighter blue berries try the form *C. t. fargesii*.

Decaisnea fargesii
Height: 2·1-3m (7-10ft)
A deciduous shrub with large 60-90cm (2-3ft) long leaves formed of thirteen to twenty-five leaflets; the mid-summer yellow-green flowers are followed by metallic-blue broad-bean-like fruits, 7·5-10cm (3-4in) long and 1·8cm (¾in) wide.

Viburnum davidii
Height: 75cm-1m (2½-3½ft)
A distinctive evergreen shrub with 5-7·5cm (2-3in) wide flat heads of white flowers in mid-summer, followed by turquoise-blue berries; both male and female plants must be present for the production of berries.

Above: **Perovskia atriplicifolia**
The violet-blue flower spikes of this hardy perennial dominate the centre of this predominantly blue herbaceous border.

Above: **Aster thompsonii nanus**
This lovely 20cm (8in) high rock garden plant produces masses of star-like lavender blue flowers set off by grey-green leaves.

Key:
1 *Picea pungens* 'Thomsen'
2 *Pinus sylvestris* 'Aurea'
3 *Picea pungens* 'Globosa'
4 *Hydrangea macrophylla*
5 *Salix* x *chrysocoma*

6 *Cotinus coggygria* 'Notcutt's Variety'
7 *Robinia pseudoacacia* 'Frisia'
8 *Chamaecyparis lawsoniana* 'Columnaris'
9 *Cedrus deodara* 'Golden Horizon'
10 *Juniperus chinensis* 'Pyramidalis'

CHAPTER ONE

THE FLOWER BORDER

Blue-flowered plants are not renowned for their winter and spring blooms, and it is usually the start of summer before their impact becomes apparent. Of course, as with every generalization, there are exceptions, like the rosy-purple *Rhododendron praecox* and other related species that show their colours in late winter and early spring. But for the main burst of blue, mauve and purple flowers, we have to wait for early summer, though there is then the reward of enjoying these colours right through to late autumn.

Asters are especially famed for late summer and autumn flower colour. Indeed, *Aster novae angliae* and *Aster novi belgii* are popularly known as Michaelmas Daisies because they flower on Michaelmas Day, the 29th of September. The flowers are usually still in bloom on Old Michaelmas Day, the 10th of October. Introduced into England during the early 1700s, these asters had particular significance in the calendar of many agricultural workers during recent centuries, because their flowering time coincided with the statute sessions, when wage rates were fixed.

The number of blue, mauve or purple hardy herbaceous perennials is large, ranging from the popular, upright Purple Cone Flower, *Echinacea purpurea*, to the reliable dahlias of autumn, treasured as much for cut flowers as for garden colour. Dahlias vary enormously in size and shape, and their classification is given in detail in this chapter, on pages 24-26. Such is the fascination of dahlias that each year we are blessed with new varieties, some to last generations and to become part of a flower enthusiast's vocabulary, while others soon pass into obscurity.

Single theme blue borders have immediate impact, thanks to their originality and eye-catching qualities, but they can often be enhanced further with patches of demure white or delicate pale lemon-yellow (but not of blinding bright yellow, which commands too much attention in full sunlight and suppresses the beauty of pastel blue tints).

Colours, though, are a personal and often intimate choice. If blue, mauve or violet are your treasured colours, then the plants in this and the following four chapters are bound to appeal to you.

Left: **Delphinium 'Thunderstorm'**, *with its startling blue spires, creates a dominant display in both herbaceous and mixed borders. Its tall stems should be tied to strong stakes.*

THE FLOWER BORDER

Above: **Agapanthus praecox**
This half-hardy evergreen creates dense 5-7·5cm (2-3in) wide heads of pale blue flowers during mid to late summer.

Agapanthus x 'Headbourne Hybrids'

African Lily (UK)

This popular hybrid is hardier than most other species. Like its relatives, it has long, strap-like mid-green leaves, with stunningly attractive deep violet-blue to pale blue flowers held in large heads like upturned umbrellas during mid to late summer.
Height: 60-75cm (2-2½ft)
Spread: 45-60cm (1½-2ft)
Cultivation: Fertile, well-drained soil and a sheltered position are needed. The foliage dies down in autumn, with fresh leaves appearing in spring. Ensure that the soil is not waterlogged during winter.
Propagation: The easiest way to increase it is by lifting and dividing established clumps in late spring, just as the new growth makes an appearance.

Right: **Agapanthus x 'Headbourne Hybrids'**
A beautiful hardy herbaceous plant, but it does not like water-saturated soil during winter. The flowers, borne in inverted umbrella-like arrangements, appear on stout stems during mid to late summer.

Aconitum wilsonii

Monkshood · Wolf's Bane · Helmet Flower (UK)
Aconite · Monkshood (USA)

This erect hardy herbaceous plant has deeply divided dark green leaves and 5cm (2in) high amethyst-blue hooded flowers during late summer and into early autumn. Several varieties are available, including 'Kelmscott Variety' (lavender-blue) and 'Barker's Variety' (deep blue).
Height: 1·2-1·8m (4-6ft)
Spread: 45-60cm (1½-2ft)
Cultivation: Deep, fertile, moisture-retentive soil in slight shade suits it best. Do not allow the soil to dry out,

Above: **Aconitum wilsonii**
A stately and erect herbaceous perennial, displaying amethyst-blue hooded flowers during late summer and into autumn. It gets one of its common names, Wolf's Bane, from its poisonous roots.

and cut the plants down to soil-level during autumn.
Propagation: It is easily increased by lifting and dividing established clumps in spring or autumn. Seeds can be sown in boxes of loam-based compost in spring and placed in a cold frame, but this method takes a couple of years to produce flowering-sized plants that will create a worthwhile, dominant display.

Aconitum napellus is another Monkshood, with deep-blue flowers during mid-summer. It blends well with a backcloth of the Venetian Sumach or Smoke Tree, *Cotinus coggygria* 'Foliis Purpureis'.

Agapanthus blends well with yellow-flowered and silver-foliaged plants. For silver foliage choose *Stachys lanata*, while *Achillea filipendula* 'Coronation Gold' with its flat flower heads provides an ample splash of yellow.

Ageratum houstonianum

(Ageratum mexicanum)

A half-hardy annual with mid-green, hairy, heart-shaped leaves and 7·5-10cm (3-4in) wide clusters of powdery bluish-mauve flowers from early to late summer. Several superb forms are grown, including 'Blue Cap' and 'Blue Danube'.

Height: 13-30cm (5-12in)
Spread: 20-30cm (8-12in)
Cultivation: Moisture-retentive soil is best, and a position in full sun or partial shade. Do not set the plants in heavy shade. Removing the dead flower heads helps to extend the flowering season, and this is especially important where the plants are being grown in containers on a patio.
Propagation: During late winter and early spring, sow seeds thinly 3mm (⅛in) deep in pots of loam-based seed compost kept at 10°C (50°F). When the seedlings are large enough to handle, prick them off into boxes and harden them off in a cold frame. Plant them out when all risk of frost has passed.

Below: **Ageratum houstonianum 'Adriatic Blue'**
A well-known half-hardy annual for summer-bedding schemes. It is especially eye-catching as a border edging and looks good alongside gravel paths.

Ageratum houstonianum can be used in many bedding combinations. Try an edging of ageratum with a carpeting of orange or salmon antirrhinums and dot plants of *Abutilon striatum* (*A. thompsonii*).

THE FLOWER BORDER

Above: **Anchusa azurea**
The beautiful blue flowers appear during mid-summer, creating a strong colour impact. The plants need support from twiggy sticks inserted at an early stage so that they can grow up through them.

Anchusa azurea

Alkanet · Italian Bugloss (UK and USA)

A brightly coloured hardy herbaceous perennial with lance-shaped mid-green leaves, rough and hairy stems, and large bright blue flowers similar to forget-me-nots displayed in large heads during mid-summer. There are several superb varieties, including 'Morning Glory' (bright blue), 'Opal' (soft blue), 'Royal Blue' (rich royal blue) and 'Loddon Royalist' (gentian-blue).
Height: 90cm-1·5m (3-5ft)
Spread: 45-60cm (1½-2ft)
Cultivation: Deep, fertile, well-drained soil in a sunny position is best. Anchusas need support from twiggy sticks; in autumn cut down the stems to soil-level.
Propagation: It is easily increased from root-cuttings. These are best taken in winter, cutting the roots into 5cm (2in) long pieces. At the stem end of each cutting make a flat cut at right-angles to the stem, while at the root end form a slanting cut. This helps to sort out the cuttings if they become mixed up. Insert them flat end upwards in pots or boxes of loam-based compost, and put them in a cold frame.

Aster amellus

Italian Starwort (UK)
Italian Aster (USA)

This well-known herbaceous perennial from Italy displays rough-surfaced grey-green leaves and 5-6·5cm (2-2½in) wide daisy-like flowers with golden-yellow centres during late summer and into autumn. Several superb forms are available, including 'King George' (soft blue-violet), 'Nocturne' (lavender-pink), 'Sonia' (large and pink) and 'Violet Queen' (compact and dwarf).
Height: 45-60cm (1½-2ft)
Spread: 38-45cm (15-18in)
Cultivation: Well-drained but moisture-retentive soil and a sunny position suit it best. It dislikes excessive water during autumn and winter. In late autumn, cut down the stems to soil-level.
Propagation: Dividing established clumps in spring is the easiest method of increasing this plant. Alternatively, take basal cuttings.

Below: **Aster amellus 'King George'**
A large-flowered aster, this variety has remained popular since it was first bred in 1914. It displays soft blue-violet flowers with dramatically contrasting golden-yellow centres.

Anchusa azurea looks spectacular when grown against a backcloth of yellow foliage, such as that of the Golden Privet (*Ligustrum ovalifolium* 'Aureum'). Lady's Mantle (*Alchemilla mollis*) is small enough to be set around the front of the anchusa.

Asters are among the brightest flowering plants in our gardens, and suit bold plantings in a herbaceous or mixed border. A few asters are small enough to be planted in a rock garden setting, such as *Aster alpinus* which is only 15cm (6in) tall.

Above: **Aster amellus 'Nocturne'**
This is an especially good form that has a compact and bushy habit with semi-double lavender-pink flowers. Free-draining soil is essential for this late summer and autumn-flowering plant to produce a good display. Unfortunately, in areas of high rainfall the flowers tend to become sodden with water and to be weighed down. This can be prevented by covering the flowerheads with a tent of plastic sheeting.

Aster x frikartii

This brightly-coloured hybrid aster between *A. amellus* and *A. thomsonii* reveals 5cm (2in) wide blue daisy-like flowers with orange centres during late summer and well into autumn. The variety 'Mönch' produces masses of clear lavender-blue flowers with yellow rayed centres.
Height: 75cm (2½ft)
Spread: 38-45cm (15-18in)

Above: **Aster x frikartii 'Mönch'**
A superb hybrid aster bearing lavender-blue flowers during late summer and into autumn, it is useful for providing colour earlier than Aster amellus varieties.

Cultivation: Fertile, well-drained soil and a sunny position suit this flower. Dry soil in late summer spells doom, but at the same time excessive wetness from ill-drained soils is also detrimental. Despite its height it does not need staking. In autumn, cut the flowered stems down to soil-level. *Aster x frikartii* blends well with late-flowering plants; some combinations are given at the base of the page. For a really stunning arrangement, use a mixture of *Anemone x hybrida* 'September Charm' with clear pink flowers, *Aster x frikartii* 'Mönch' and the pink *Nerine bowdenii* 'Fenwick's Variety'. Set these in front of the Chinese shrub *Hydrangea villosa*, which bears loose heads of pale purple flowers in late summer and early autumn. Even a single combination of *Aster x frikartii* 'Mönch' and the white *Anemone x hybrida* 'Honorine Jobert' looks lovely.
Propagation: Dividing established clumps in spring is the easiest method of increasing this plant. Alternatively, take basal cuttings in spring and put them in a frame.

Aster x **frikartii** is useful in herbaceous or mixed borders, and can be grown with many other plants, such as *Anemone* x *hybrida*, *Nerine bowdenii* 'Fenwick's Variety', *Acanthus mollis* and *Sedum maximum* 'Atropurpureum'.

THE FLOWER BORDER

Borago officinalis

Borage (UK)
Talewort · Cool-tankard (USA)

This is a hardy annual, well-known as a culinary herb, with leaves used when young and fresh to flavour salads and fruit cups. They have a flavour reminiscent of cucumber, and are large, oval, green and covered with hairs. The five-petalled, blue, 18-25mm (¾-1in) wide flowers appear in pendulous clusters from mid-summer onwards. White and purple forms are also available.
Height: 45-90cm (1½-3ft)
Spread: 30-38cm (12-15in)
Cultivation: Although this plant will grow in most soils, it does better in well-drained ground in a sunny position. It is well su 'ed to a sunny bank or for a warm mixed border.
Propagation: During spring, sow seeds in shallow drills where the plants are to flower. When they are large enough to handle, thin the seedlings to 25-30cm (10-12in) apart for strong, healthy growth.

Campanula lactiflora

Milky Bellflower (UK)

This beautiful hardy herbaceous perennial has stems smothered in small light green leaves. The miniature bell-like light lavender-blue flowers appear during mid-summer. There is a wide range of varieties, including 'Prichard's Variety' at 90cm (3ft) with lavender-blue flowers, 'Loddon Anna' at 1-1·2m (3½-4ft) with flesh-pink flowers, and 'Pouffe' at 25cm (10in) with light lavender-blue flowers.
Cultivation: Fertile deeply-cultivated and well-drained soil in full sun or slight shade suits it. But ensure that the soil does not dry out during summer. The tall-growing varieties

Borago officinalis, like many other seed-raised culinary and medicinal herbs, can be used in mixed borders or in odd corners, especially when a separate herb garden cannot be given entirely to them.

Below: **Campanula lactiflora 'Pouffe'**
A beautiful dwarf and hummock-forming campanula with light lavender-blue flowers during mid-summer. Other forms of this campanula rise to 90cm-1·5m (3-5ft).

need support in exposed areas.
Propagation: The easiest way to increase it is by division of large clumps during spring or autumn. Alternatively, take 4-5cm (1½-2in) long cuttings in spring, inserting them in pots of equal parts peat and sharp sand and placing these in a cold frame. When the plants are well grown, set them into their permanent positions in the garden. Alternatively, grow on the plants in a nursery bed before final planting.

Campanula medium

Canterbury Bell (UK and USA)

Most gardeners know this lovely old hardy biennial, with an upright stance and 2·5-4cm (1-1½in) long bell-shaped blue, pink, white or purple flowers from late spring to mid-summer. The best known form is the so-called Cup-and-Saucer variety, 'Calycanthema'. 'Bells of Holland', 38cm (15in) high and with a conical growth habit, has a mixture of single flowers in shades of blue, mauve, rose and white. Another form, 38-50cm (15-20in) high, is 'Dwarf Musical Bells' with multi-coloured bell-like flowers smothering the plants in blue, white and pink.
Height: 45-90cm (1½-3ft)

Above: **Campanula medium**
This reliable old favourite hardy biennial should find a place in any garden. It is ideal for filling bare areas in mixed borders, or as a high edging to paths.

Spread: 38-45cm (15-18in)
Cultivation: Moderately rich, well-drained soil in a sunny position suits this lovely plant.
Propagation: From spring to early summer, sow seeds 6mm (¼in) deep in a prepared seedbed. After germination and when large enough to handle, thin the seedlings to 23cm (9in) apart. During autumn, plant them into their flowering positions when the soil is in a workable condition.

White or yellow-flowered plants look superb with this blue herbaceous perennial. The tall-growing forms blend well with *Lilium regale* and the Madonna Lily, *Lilium candidum*. They can also join shape-contrasting but similarly-coloured plants to create blue textures.

Campanula medium is ideal grown as bold clumps in a mixed border, where it will bring colour while permanent plants are developing, perhaps blending with other ephemeral plants such as Love-in-a-mist *Nigella damascena* and Candytuft. *Iberis umbellata*.

THE FLOWER BORDER

Above: **Centaurea moschata 'Dobies Giant'**
An easily-grown hardy annual bringing large fragrant flowers in pastel tints to the garden from early summer to autumn.

Centaurea moschata

(Centaurea imperialis)
Sweet Sultan (UK and USA)

This beautiful plant, native to the Eastern Mediterranean, is grown as a hardy annual. From early summer to autumn it displays sweetly-scented cornflower-like flowers in shades of purple, pink, white or yellow. The flowers, up to 7·5cm (3in) wide, are borne above the narrow grey-green leaves that display toothed edges. Another, more commonly grown relative is the Cornflower or Bluebottle, a native of Europe, with bright blue flowers.
Height: 45-60cm (1½-2ft)
Spread: 25-30cm (10-12in)
Cultivation: Fertile well-drained garden soil and full sun suit it. Removing dead flower heads helps to prolong the lives of the plants. In exposed areas they will need support from twiggy sticks.
Propagation: During spring, sow seeds where they are to flower. Set them in shallow drills, thinning the seedlings to 23cm (9in) apart when they are large enough to handle.

Ceratostigma plumbaginoides

This hardy sub-shrubby perennial from Western China has wide lance-shaped mid-green leaves that become tinged with red during autumn. The terminal clusters of blue flowers appear from late summer onwards, and it is a useful plant for bringing late colour to rock gardens and mixed borders.
Height: 25-30cm (10-12in)
Spread: 30-38cm (12-15in)
Cultivation: Light soil and an open but slightly sheltered position suit this attractive plant.
Propagation: It is easily increased by lifting and dividing clumps in spring, just before shoots appear.

Above: **Centaurea cyanus 'Tall Double Mixed'**
This hardy annual is very reliable and seldom fails to create a dominant display with its striking flowers in shades of blue, maroon, red, rose and white from early summer to autumn. It rises to about 90cm (3ft) high if the soil is kept moist, slightly less than this in dry conditions. In England it is known as the Cornflower, and in North America as the Bluebottle.

Below: **Ceratostigma plumbaginoides**
A pretty, hardy sub-shrub, ideal for late blue colour in a rock garden. Its foliage is a delight in autumn, when tinged with red, and it looks superb positioned at the base of a wall.

Centaurea moschata is a delight in an annual border, where its flowers can be used alongside many other hardy annuals without any fear of its colour dominating its neighbours. It is good for cut flowers, so plant it within arm's length of scissors.

Ceratostigma willmottianum is a half-hardy deciduous shrub with diamond-shaped stalkless leaves. It bears terminal clusters of small rich blue flowers during mid-summer, and is ideal in a mixed border or even in a herbaceous mixture.

Left: **Chelone obliqua**
An attractive herbaceous perennial with snapdragon-like flowers during late summer. This North American plant can often be invasive when established, spreading rapidly.

Chelone obliqua

Turtle-head (UK)
Turtlehead · Snakehead (USA)

This interesting, rather curious-looking hardy herbaceous perennial has 2·5cm (1in) long deep rose snapdragon-like flowers during late summer. These are borne on stiff, erect stems, from joints also bearing dark green lance-shaped leaves with serrated edges. *Chelone lyonii*, another North American native, is a hardy herbaceous perennial with terminal clusters of 2·5cm (1in) long pink flowers from mid summer to early autumn. The plant eventually rises to about 75-90cm (2½-3ft) high.
Height: 60-75cm (2-2½ft)
Spread: 30-38cm (12-15in)
Cultivation: Fertile, light, well-drained soil is needed, together with a position in full sun or light shade. In wind-protected gardens it may not require support from twiggy sticks, but in cold and exposed areas this becomes essential. In autumn cut down the stems to soil-level.
Propagation: It is easily increased by division of the roots during spring or autumn, replanting only the young parts from around the outside of the clump. Alternatively, seeds can be sown under glass in 15°C (59°F) in early spring. Using this method takes two years to produce flowering-sized plants.

Left: **Ceratostigma willmottianum**
This hardy deciduous shrub is quite similar to Ceratostigma plumbagi-noides *(far left). However, C. will-mottianum has lance-shaped leaves. The small, rich blue flowers are borne in terminal clusters from mid-summer to autumn, and the leaves turn red in autumn. It grows best in the shelter of a warm wall; in spring, cut out old, dead or damaged shoots to soil level. You can trim the entire plant to make this job easier.*

Chelone obliqua is best planted in a mixed or herbaceous border, alongside colour-contrasting and vigorous herbaceous plants such as the Shasta Daisy, *Chrysanthemum maximum.*

THE FLOWER BORDER

Above: **Dahlia 'Gypsy Dance'**
A bedding variety, ideal for the front of a border or in bedding schemes during summer. The small highly-coloured flowers are available in single and double forms.

Dahlias

These fast-growing garden favourites can be divided into two main groups: those grown as half-hardy annuals for use in bedding schemes; and those that are best in mixed borders, mingled with herbaceous plants.

BEDDING DAHLIAS
These half-hardy perennials from Mexico are grown as half-hardy annuals, displaying 5-7·5cm (2-3in) wide single, double or semi-double flowers from mid-summer to autumn. There are many varieties in a wide colour range, in mixed or self-colours.
Height: 30-50cm (12-20in)
Spread: 38-45cm (15-24in)
Cultivation: Well-cultivated, fertile, compost or manure-enriched soil and a sunny position suit bedding dahlias. Soil too rich, however, will create excessive foliage at the expense of flowers. There is no need to stake them, unlike the larger border types. The removal of dead flowers assists in the development of

further blooms. Water the plants during dry periods.
Propagation: During the late winter and early summer sow seeds 6mm (¼in) deep in a loam-based seed compost at 16°C (61°F). When they are large enough to handle, prick off the seedlings into boxes or small pots of loam-based compost and slowly harden them off in a cold frame. Set the plants out in the garden as soon as all risk of frost has passed.

Above: **Dahlia 'Kay Helen'**
A ball type with very neat and compact blooms that look equally good in the garden or cut and displayed in a vase indoors. Dahlias thrive in rich soil and need a sunny position. The globular flowers are produced on stiff stems that with this variety carry the flowers above the foliage. To encourage rapid growth the soil must be carefully enriched before planting with the addition of bulky well-rotted compost or manure, worked in well with a fork.

Ball-type dahlias in England can be traced back to a nursery in Hammersmith, London in about 1818. The nursery, owned by Mr. T. Lee, received tubers from France and included early forms of ball types.

Left: **Dahlia 'Earl Marc'**
A distinctive semi-cactus, not as quilled or tubular as the cactus types. The flowers have flatter petals.

BORDER DAHLIAS

These half-hardy tuberous plants, though easily damaged by frost, are unsurpassed for bringing colour to a garden quickly. There are several classifications and many varieties. Indeed, each year hundreds of new varieties are introduced by dahlia specialists, while others are no longer marketed. When the dahlia was first grown as an exhibition flower in the early 1800s it consisted solely of ball types. To indicate their value, some new varieties were sold for as much as a guinea. At first no classification was recognized for the ball types, or for various other types of dahlia that were produced. However, catalogues were soon issued by traders in dahlias and these contained a rough classification. In 1904 the British National Dahlia Society in conjunction with the Joint Dahlia Committee published a classified list called the Classification and Description of Dahlias.

Anemone-flowered (60cm-1m/ 2-3½ft): These have double flowers with flat outer petals and short, tubular inner ones. Flowering is from mid summer to the frosts of autumn.

Ball-type (90cm/3ft): As implied, these have ball-shaped flowers, with tubular petals displaying blunt ends. There are *Small Ball* types with blooms 10-15cm (4-6in) wide, and *Miniature Ball* forms with flowers up to 10cm (4in) wide.

Cactus and Semi-cactus (90cm- 1·5m/3-5ft): These are divided into five groupings— *Miniature* (blooms up to 10cm/4in wide); *Small* (blooms 10-15cm/4-6in wide); *Medium* (blooms 15-20cm/6-8in wide); *Large* (blooms 20-25cm/8-10in wide); and *Giant* (blooms 25cm/10in or more wide). Cactus types have petals rolled back or quilled for more than half their length. Semi-cactus types have similar petals, but quilled or rolled back for less than half of their total length.

Dwarf dahlias are thought to have been developed from low-growing forms found in 1750 on the lower slopes of the Sierra del Ajusca mountains in Mexico. The plants were said to be about 38-45cm (15-18in) high.

THE FLOWER BORDER

Collarette (75cm-1·m/2½-4ft): These have blooms with a single outer ring of flat ray florets and a ring of small florets in the centre, forming a disc.
Decorative: These have double flowers without central discs. They are formed of broad, flat ray florets. This grouping is subdivided into:
Miniature (90cm-1·2m/3-4ft): these have flowers up to 10cm (4in) wide.
Small (1-1·2m/3½-4ft): flowers 10-15cm (4-6in) wide.
Medium (1-1·2m/3-4ft): flowers 15-20cm (6-8in) wide.
Large (1-1·5m/3½-5ft): flowers 20-25cm (8-10in) wide.
Giant (1·2-1·5m/4-5ft): flowers 25cm (10in) or more wide.
Paeony-flowered (up to 90cm/3ft): flowers formed of two or more rings of flat ray florets, with a central disc.
Pompon (90cm-1·2m/3-4ft): flowers closely resemble those of *Ball* types, but are more globular and do not exceed 5cm (2in) wide. The florets curls inwards for their entire length.
Single-flowered (45-75cm/1½-2½ft): flowers up to 10cm (4in) wide, with a single row of petals arranged round a central disc.
Cultivation: Well-drained soil, with plenty of moisture-retentive compost

or well-decomposed manure added, is required. Add a sprinkling of bonemeal before setting the tubers 10cm (4in) deep in the soil during mid to late spring. If you are planting sprouted tubers, take care that you do not plant them too early, as frost will damage them. The plants will need staking. Nip out the growing tips of all shoots to encourage sideshoots to develop. If you want large flowers, remove sideshoots and buds from around the developing flowers. Removing dead flowers helps in the development of further blooms. In autumn gently dig up the tubers about a week after the foliage has been blackened by frost. Remove soil from the tubers and store them upside down for a few

Left: **Dahlia 'Scaur Princess'**
A beautifully-coloured decorative type which brings distinction to any garden.

Dahlias are superb for filling large blank areas in mixed borders, where they create spectacular colourful displays during late summer and into early autumn until frosts damage them. They are soon blackened by frost.

Left: **Dahlia 'Vicky Jackson'**
A decorative cactus, producing masses of flowers from mid-summer onwards until the frosts of late autumn.

Right: **Dahlia 'Willo's Violet'**
A beautiful pompon type, with deep violet flowers and a height of about 1m (3½ft). It is excellent as an exhibition dahlia.

weeks to dry them out. Then place them in boxes of peat in a dry, frost-proof position until the following year.
Propagation: The easiest way for the home gardener to do this is to divide the tubers in spring.
Dahlias in floral art: As well as creating colour in the garden the flowers of dahlias are ideal for decorating the home. The art of presenting dahlias for room decoration is not difficult, and part of the skill in using them relies on the choice of colours. Blue flowers, whatever their tone, need to be carefully used as the colour tends to fade in artificial light. Purples and mauves, however, can be used subtly, especially where they echo the same tones in the room. However, when used with white-flowered dahlias, which both lighten and dramatize the arrangement, the effect can be quite different. In contrast, other colours such as yellow and orange are much warmer and radiate a strong feeling of cheerfulness. Those flowers rich in scarlet, however, can create the effect of warmth in rooms facing east and north and not subjected to strong summer sunshine. Rooms facing north or east generally benefit from warm colours, such as orange, scarlet, yellow and amber, whereas cool colours such as pale mauve, lilac-pink, purple shades and lavender are better in south and west-facing rooms. If strong-coloured blooms are used they can be given even greater impact by mixing them with pastel-coloured flowers.

Collarette type dahlias originated in the municipal gardens of the Parc de la Tete d'Or at Lyons, France, during the last years of the last century. Specimens of these plants arrived in Britain in 1901.

THE FLOWER BORDER

Left: **Echinacea purpurea**
This stately herbaceous perennial is justifiably famous for its richly coloured flowers, from mid-summer to autumn. The cone-like orange centres to the flowers are a particularly attractive feature.

Echinacea purpurea

Purple Cone Flower (UK and USA)

A well-known hardy herbaceous perennial, formerly called *Rudbeckia purpurea*. Its upright stems bear purple-crimson daisy-like flowers, 10cm (4in) wide, at their tops from mid to late summer. The lance-shaped, dark green leaves are slightly toothed and rough to the touch. Several superb varieties are

Echinacea purpurea is a dominant flower, with the erect stems often holding the flowers high above neighbouring plants, like islands of colour. Surrounding plants should have subdued colours.

available, including 'Robert Bloom' (carmine-purple), 'The King' (crimson-purple) and 'White Lustre' (white petalled with deep orange centres).

Height: 90cm-1·2m (3-4ft)
Spread: 60-75cm (2-2½ft)
Cultivation: Well-drained fertile soil and a sunny position are essential for success. Set the plants in position in spring, and in autumn cut their stems down to soil-level.
Propagation: Although it can be increased from seeds sown in spring at 13°C (55°F), division of established clumps during spring or autumn is a much easier method. Use only the young parts from around the outside of the clump for replanting in the border.

Above: **Echinops ritro**
This hardy herbaceous perennial is highly cherished by flower arrangers. The globular flower heads appear during mid-summer and last a long time after cutting.

Left: **Echium plantagineum 'Monarch Dwarf Hybrids'**
A hardy dwarf mixture, up to 30cm (1ft) high, these hybrids produce flowers in many pastel tints. When grown in a sunny position, they seldom fail to attract bees.

Echinops ritro

Globe Thistle (UK)
Small Globe Thistle (USA)

This hardy herbaceous perennial has deep green, thistle-like leaves and round, 4-5cm (1½-2in) wide, steel-blue flowers held on stiff stems during mid-summer. Bees find the flowers especially attractive.
Height: 90cm-1·2m (3-4ft)
Spread: 60-75cm (2-2½ft)
Cultivation: Most soils are suitable, but they should be well-drained and in full sun. This is a plant that is self-supporting and therefore ideal for island beds. During autumn, cut the plant down to soil-level.
Propagation: It can be increased from root-cuttings taken in late autumn, inserted in sandy compost and placed in a cold frame before

planting out in the garden. But the division of established clumps in spring or autumn is a much easier and quicker method.

Echium plantagineum

(Echium lycopsis)
Viper's Bugloss (UK and USA)

This distinctive hardy annual from Europe has mid-green leaves and upturned blue or pale purple bell-shaped flowers from mid-summer onwards. Although it normally grows up to 90cm (3ft), several lower-growing forms at 30cm (1ft) are available, including 'Blue Bedder' and 'Monarch Dwarf Hybrids' with blue, pink, lavender and white flowers. Several other species of echium can be grown in the garden, including the bushy, hardy biennial *Echium rubrum*. From early to mid-summer it displays 12mm (½in) long bright red tubular flowers with eye-catching yellow stamens. Another species, *Echium vulgare*, the Common Viper's Bugloss is a hardy biennial, but is invariably grown as an annual. It is relatively short (60cm/2ft high) bushy and compact and bears tubular, 12mm (½in) long, purple-budded, violet flowers from mid to late summer. *Echium vulgare* and *Echium plantagineum* are both natives of the British Isles. *E. vulgare* is found in grassy places on light soils near the coast, while *E. plantagineum* grows in sandy areas near the sea, in the South-west.
Height: 75-90cm (2½-3ft)
Spread: 45cm (1½ft)
Cultivation: Light, dry soil and a sunny position are needed, although partial shade also suits it.
Propagation: During spring, sow seeds 6mm (¼in) deep in their flowering positions, thinning the seedlings to 15cm (6in) apart. Seeds can also be sown in autumn, but wait until spring before thinning them. For earlier flowers, sow seeds in loam-based seed compost in late winter or early spring at 13°C (55°F). Prick out the seedlings into boxes when they are large enough to handle, and harden them off before planting them out.

Echinops ritro is best planted in large clumps, where its dominant flower heads blend with a background grouping of *Campanula lactiflora* with small bell-shaped light lavender-blue flowers.

Echium plantagineum in one of its dwarf forms is of greater use in a garden than taller types. It is ideally suited for annual borders, and also for bringing height and shape contrast to small ornamental grasses.

THE FLOWER BORDER

Eryngium bourgatii

Sea Holly (UK)
Eryngo (USA)

This hardy herbaceous perennial has stiff, upright and branching bluish stems bearing spiny, holly-like leaves and silver-blue, thistle-shaped flower heads during mid to late summer.

Height: 38-45cm (15-18in)
Spread: 30-38cm (12-15in)
Cultivation: It grows best in fertile well-drained soil in a sunny location. Only in exposed areas will it need support from twiggy sticks. In autumn, cut down the plant to soil-level.
Propagation: It can be increased by taking root cuttings in autumn and inserting them in pots of equal parts peat and sharp sand. Place them in a cold frame during winter and set the plants out into their permanent sites in the garden when they are well-grown.

Right: **Eryngium bourgatii**
This hardy herbaceous perennial displays strikingly attractive foliage and flower heads, much cherished by flower arrangers for home decoration.

Below right: **Eupatorium purpureum 'Atropurpureum'**
This exciting hardy and reliable herbaceous perennial with purplish foliage and rosy-lilac flowers is admirable for mixed or herbaceous borders, as well as wild gardens.

Eupatorium purpureum

Joe Pye Weed (UK)
Joe-pye Weed · Sweet Joe-pye Weed · Green-stemmed Joe-pye Weed (USA)

This handsome upright hardy herbaceous perennial from North America has purplish stems bearing slender and pointed mid-green leaves. Fluffy, branching, 10-13cm (4-5in) wide heads of rose-purple flowers are borne from mid to late summer. The form 'Atropurpureum' bears rosy-lilac flowers and purplish leaves.

There are several other superb **Sea Hollies**, including *Eryngium alpinum*, with frilled collars around the bases of its steel-blue flower heads, and *E.* x *oliverianum* which is graced with deep blue heads.

Eupatorium purpureum is a dominant plant, often standing above its neighbours. In a mixed border, its height and colour create a pleasing combination with the blue *Hydrangea macrophylla*.

Height: 1·2-1·8m (4-6ft)
Spread: 75-90cm (2½-3ft)
Cultivation: Any good relatively moisture-retentive and fertile soil suits it, in full sun or light shade. During autumn cut down the stems to soil-level. It benefits from a mulch with well-rotted manure or garden compost every spring. Before applying it, however, hoe the surface to remove all weeds.
Propagation: It is easily increased by lifting and dividing established clumps in autumn or spring.

Left: **Festuca glauca**
This densely-tufted perennial grass is ideal for the front of a border. To create an impressive clump, use three or five plants, each 20cm (8in) apart.

Festuca glauca

Sheep's Fescue · Blue Fescue (UK and USA)

This hardy perennial grass forms a striking clump of bristle-like blue-grey leaves. It is ideal for planting at the edge of a border, where it can be used to soft harsh edges, and blends well with gravel paths. During summer it is adorned with oval, purple spikelets of flowers.
Height: 20-25cm (8-10in)
Spread: 15-20cm (6-8in)
Cultivation: Well-drained light soil and a sunny position are best.
Propagation: Seeds can be sown in a sheltered border, planting the seedlings out into a nursery bed when they are large enough to handle. It is generally easier, however, to lift and divide large clumps in spring or autumn.

Filipendula purpurea

(Spiraea palmata)

A handsome though dominating hardy herbaceous perennial with large lobed leaves held on crimson stems and surmounted by large flat heads of small carmine-rose flowers during mid-summer.
Height: 75cm-1·2m (2½-4ft)
Spread: 75-90cm (2½-3ft) and more
Cultivation: An ideal plant for rich, fertile, moisture-retentive soil in partial shade, perhaps in a wild garden or at the side of an informal garden pond.
Propagation: It is easily increased by lifting and dividing large clumps in autumn or spring.

Left: **Filipendula purpurea**
An impressive herbaceous perennial for a fertile, moist, cool position in slight shade. Its carmine-rose flower heads form a dominant display during mid-summer.

Festuca glauca is superb for a colour contrast with yellow-flowered plants, such as Golden Garlic *Allium moly*, which is also known as Yellow Onion. Position the grass in front of the allium.

Filipendula rubra is another attractive filipendula, with large pinkish flower heads up to 28cm (11in) across. It is widely grown in the form 'Venusta' with deep pink flowers. It loves moist soil and slight shade.

THE FLOWER BORDER

Gladiolus byzantinus

Sword Lily (UK)

This hardy and reliable gladiolus has 25-38cm (10-15in) long flower spikes loosely packed with up to twenty plum-coloured 6·5in) wide blooms during mid-summer. The narrow, sword-like and upright ribbed leaves with pointed tops rise to 60cm (2ft).
Height: 60cm (2ft)
Spread: 13-18cm (5-7in)
Cultivation: Rich, fertile, well-drained but moisture-retentive soil and full sun suit it best. The corms can be left in the soil from year to year, and in light soils it is best to plant them 15cm (6in) deep — 10cm (4in) in heavy soil — so that they are self-supporting and do not become blown over. In heavy soil, place a handful of sharp sand under each corm when planting it. Remove dead flower stems after flowering and cut down the yellowed foliage to soil-level in autumn — but not too early or it will not have transferred its food content to the corms, which act as storage organs to help the plants survive winter.
Propagation: Every four or five years lift the plants in autumn and remove the little cormlets attached to the corm. Dry them and replant them in spring in sand-lined drills in a nursery bed.

Above: **Gladiolus byzantinus**
This small-flowered gladiolus flowers much earlier than its large-flowered relatives. Well-drained soil and a position in full sun assure success.

Hosta rectifolia 'Tall Boy'

Plantain Lily (UK)
Plantain Lily · Day Lily (USA)

These hardy perennials with beautiful leaves, variegated in some varieties, were once known as *Funkias*. This species displays broad, lance-shaped mid to dark green leaves and tall, upright flower stems bearing 5cm (2in) long violet-mauve flowers in slender spikes during mid-summer. Several other hostas, including *H. crispula*, have purple flowers. During mid to late summer this plant reveals lilac-purple flowers above its dark green, white-edged leaves, the feature for which it is mainly grown.
Height: 1-1·3m (3½-4½ft)
Spread: 75-90cm (2½-3ft)
Cultivation: Well-drained but moisture-retentive soil enriched with leafmould and in a lightly shaded position suits it. During dry summers, it will be necessary to water the soil.
Propagation: In spring, lift and divide large clumps. This variety can be raised from seed, but variegated hostas do not come true from seed.

Hostas are among the most attractive of border flowers for naturalized or woodland settings, or even large rock gardens. The variegated types, such as *Hosta fortunei* 'Albopicta' are especially attractive.

Left: Hosta rectifolia 'Tall Boy'
This beautiful violet-mauve-flowered plant is ideal for a wild garden, where the soil does not become dry during summer. Even when not in flower, the foliage forms a dominant display, especially in early summer.

Right: Hosta 'Halcyon'
This attractively-flowered hosta creates a dominant display in a slightly-raised border, where the leaves can spread safely without being trodden upon or splashed with soil during heavy rainfall. Here it is planted against the grass Hakonechloa macra 'Albo-aurea', with narrow bronze-tinted, variegated green and buff leaves. This grass has a cascading growth habit and looks good positioned at a corner.

Iberis umbellata

Candytuft (UK)
Globe Candytuft (USA)

This well-known highly-fragrant hardy annual from Southern Europe has mid-green, pointed, narrow leaves. The 5cm (2in) wide clustered heads of purple, white and rose-red flowers appear from early summer to autumn from successive sowings. It is an annual that is well known to children and often the first plant they sow. It soon germinates and forms an edging for the side of a path. Alternatively, set it in bold drifts towards the front of a border.
Height: 15-38cm (6-15in)
Spread: 23cm (9in)
Cultivation: Well-drained, even poor soil in full sun suits it. Remove dead flower heads to extend the flowering season.
Propagation: From late spring to early summer, sow seeds in shallow drills where the plants are to flower. The seeds take ten to fourteen days to germinate. When the seedlings are large enough to handle, thin them to 20-23cm (8-9in) apart.

Right: Iberis umbellata
This easily-grown and highly fragrant hardy annual flowers over a long period from successive sowings, it is superb for planting in poor soils.

Iberis umbellata is a very amenable plant and associates with many others, such as Canterbury Bells (*Campanula medium*), Clarkia (*Clarkia elegans*) and Virginian Stock (*Malcolmia maritima*).

THE FLOWER BORDER

Incarvillea mairei

(Incarvillea grandiflora brevipes ·
I. brevipes)
Trumpet Flower (UK)

This herbaceous perennial has
attractive, deep green, pinnate leaves
and bears rich pinkish-purple
flowers with long tubular yellow
throats during early to mid-summer.
Height: 30cm (1ft)
Spread: 20-25cm (8-10in)
Cultivation: Fertile, well-drained light
soil in full sun assures success.
During spring, plant the fleshy roots
7·5cm (3in) deep, and in cold areas
protect the young and newly-
emerging shoots and leaves with a
cloche or layer of straw. In particularly
cold places they may require
protection throughout winter. Often
the new shoots are slow to emerge
from the soil in spring, so take care
not to damage them with early
spring cultivations.
Propagation: Although the crowns
can be lifted and divided in spring,
they are sometimes tough and
difficult to split. Instead, sow seeds in
a prepared seedbed in spring,
transplanting them the following
spring to their permanent positions.

Right: **Incarvillea mairei**
*This is a beautiful herbaceous
perennial for the front of a border, or
even for a rock garden where extra
height is desired. The yellow-throated
pinkish-purple flowers appear
during early to mid-summer.*

Right: **Iris douglasiana**
*This beautiful Californian iris needs
limy (alkaline) soil and forms a
large clump of colour in early
summer. The plants are often short-
lived, but can be easily raised from
seeds. The flowers are superb for
home decoration.*

Iris douglasiana

This beardless hardy iris from
California has slender, coarse, deep
green leaves that are normally
evergreen and spread out to a width
of 60cm (2ft). The 7·5cm (3in) wide
flowers are borne in fours or fives on
branched stems. They are in shades

Incarvillea delavayi is another well-known species,
rising to 60cm (2ft) and displaying 5-7·5cm
(2-3in) long rose-pink flowers during early summer.
This species is taller than *Incarvillea mairei*.

Iris douglasiana is ideal for setting around
rhododendrons, where it helps to produce ground
cover and to create colour when some of the
rhododendrons have finished flowering.

of blue-purple and lavender, with distinctive veining on the 'falls' (the three outer petals), and appear from early to mid-summer.

Height: 30-45cm (1-1½ft)

Spread: 60-75cm (2-2½ft)

Cultivation: This iris tolerates a little lime in the soil, and needs full sun or partial shade. However, it also grows well in neutral or slightly acid soil.

Propagation: It tends to be short-lived, but fortunately it is easily increased from seed sown during autumn in boxes of loam-based compost kept at 10°C (50°F). Alternatively lift and divide the rhizomes in autumn, but take care that they do not dry out before becoming established.

Iris sibirica

Siberian Iris (UK and USA)

This versatile iris is suitable for a herbaceous border as well as the margins of an informal pond. The slender, sword-like, mid-green leaves die down in winter. The flowers are about 6·5cm (2½in) wide and are borne during mid-summer. In the original species, they are in various shades of blue, with white veining on the 'falls' (the three outer petals). Because the original species hybridizes freely, usually only hybrids are available. Good ones are 'Heavenly Blue' (rich azure blue), 'Cambridge' (pale blue), 'Ottawa' (clear light blue), 'Tropic Night' (velvety violet) and 'Perry's Blue' (deep blue).

Height: 75cm-1m (2½-3½ft)

Spread: 45-60cm (1½-2ft)

Cultivation: It grows best in moist soil, but will also perform well in a herbaceous border, where it does not usually grow so high. Plant the rhizomes 2·5cm (1in) deep in the soil during autumn or spring.

Propagation: It is easily increased by lifting and dividing congested clumps in late autumn or spring. Replant the divided rhizomes 2·5cm (1in) deep. Large clumps tend to become hollow and bare at their centres, and are therefore best lifted and divided at least every four or five years to keep them healthy.

Above: **Iris sibirica 'Heavenly Blue'** *This is a hardy iris for a border or the moist margin of a pond. Its rich blue flowers are borne two or three to a stem above the grassy sword-like leaves.*

Iris sibirica, planted in a moist area, mixes well with yellow-flowered plants such as the fragrant Himalayan Cowslip, *Primula sikkimensis*, and *P. heelodoxa*. It also looks good in a border against an old wall.

THE FLOWER BORDER

Liatris spicata

Blazing Star · Gayfeather · Spike Gayfeather (UK)
Blazing Star · Button Snakeroot · Gay-feather (USA)

This hardy, tuberous-rooted, herbaceous perennial has small, strap-like, narrow, mid-green leaves. It bears dense, 15-30cm (6-12in) long, paintbrush-like spikes of pinkish-purple flowers during late summer and early autumn on stiff, leafy stems. A similar plant, *Liatris callilepis*, has bright carmine flower heads. The form 'Kobold' is even more attractive, with frothy bright carmine flower spikes, often up to 30cm (1ft) long. It grows well even on poor soil. When planted in a small grouping, it creates a superb splash of mid-summer colour. This attractive variety has the advantage of growing to only 60cm (2ft) high, whereas the original species, *Liatris callilepis*, rises to 90cm (3ft) and requires much more room, being better positioned in a flower border than in a rock garden. Another species, *Liatris graminifolia*, is not so widely grown. During late summer and into early autumn it produces purple flower spikes, surrounded by rather sparse leaves attractively covered with white spots. This species has the advantage of growing well in poor and dry soils.

Height: 60-90cm (2-3ft)
Spread: 38-45cm (15-18in)
Cultivation: Ordinary garden soil — not too heavy — and a position in full sun suit the Blazing Star.
Propagation: During spring lift and divide established clumps. To ensure the clumps are readily identified, mark them in autumn. Alternatively, wait until late spring before dividing them, when the young shoots will be apparent.

Left: **Liatris callilepis 'Kobold'**
The frothy flowers of this tuberous-rooted herbaceous perennial are a delight during mid-summer to early autumn. The flowers are useful for home decoration.

Liatris spicata is ideal for the front of a mixed or herbaceous border. Suitable companions include Red Hot Pokers (*Kniphofia*), *Bergenia* 'Silberlicht' and the Oregon Grape *Mahonia aquifolium*.

Above: **Liriope muscari**
This hardy perennial displays deep green, arching, grass-like leaves throughout the year. The lilac-mauve flowers appear from late summer through to late autumn. They bear some resemblance to those of Grape Hyacinths. As an added bonus, the leaves remain attractive throughout the year.

Linum narbonense

Flax (UK and USA)

This well-known hardy perennial has narrow, lance-shaped, grey-green leaves and graceful, arching stems that usually die back in winter in colder climates but may persist throughout winter in milder regions. The 2·5-3cm (1-1¼in) wide rich blue flowers, borne at the tops of the stems, appear throughout the summer months. *Linum perenne* is another hardy and perennial flax, rising to 30-45cm (1-1½ft). It has narrow lance-shaped greyish-green leaves and 2·5cm (1in) wide sky-blue flowers during mid to late summer. Like *Linum narbonense* it is also short-lived, but can be easily raised from seed. *Linum usitatissimum*, the Common Flax or Linseed, is a pale-blue-flowered hardy annual. It rises to about 60cm (2ft), with slender stems bearing 12mm (½in) wide, saucer-shaped flowers during mid-

Above: **Linum narbonense**
Although tall, this Flax is suitable for a rock garden. The flowers, borne at the ends of long stems, appear throughout summer.

summer. *Linum austriacum* is another soft-blue flowered plant, but is a hardy perennial and has 2·5cm (1in) wide heads in mid-summer.
Height: 30-60cm (1-2ft)
Spread: 30-38cm (12-15in)
Cultivation: Ordinary well-drained garden soil and a sunny position suit Flax best. It will tolerate both slightly acid and limy soil.
Propagation: During early summer, sow seeds 6mm (¼in) deep in a prepared seed bed. When the seedlings are large enough to handle, thin them to 20-23cm (8-9in) apart. In autumn, transfer them to their flowering positions. The plants are quite short-lived, so it is best to buy fresh plants every three or four years and replace old ones.

Liriope muscari

Turf Lily (UK and USA)

This hardy, compact and clump-forming evergreen perennial has dark green grass-like leaves and upright stems, which bear 7·5-13cm (3-5in) long spikes of bell-shaped, lilac-mauve flowers from late summer through to autumn. The species *Liriope spicata* is quite similar, but with more erect and narrower leaves. From late summer and into autumn it displays 5-7·5cm (2-3in) long spikes of bright mauve, bell-shaped flowers. It is slightly shorter than *Liriope muscari*, rising to a height of 38cm (15in).
Height: 30-38cm (12-15in)
Spread: 38-45cm (15-18in)
Cultivation: Well-drained light and fertile soil in full sun or slight shade suits it well. Remove the flower heads when they fade.
Propagation: During spring, lift and divide congested clumps.

Linum narbonense, with its cottage-garden appeal, is at home by the side of an old-looking flight of steps, against a weathered wall or as a perfect foil for grey-leaved plants.

Liriope muscari is ideal for the edge of a border or alongside a path. It harmonizes well with the Autumn Crocus (*Colchicum autumnale*), *Nerine bowdenii* or *Sedum* x 'Autumn Joy'.

THE FLOWER BORDER

Lupinus polyphyllus 'Russell Hybrids'

Lupin · Lupine (UK)
Lupine (USA)

These hardy herbaceous perennials are familiar to most gardeners. Their slender, upright spires of blue or red mid-summer flowers are borne above mid-green leaves formed of a circle of ten to seventeen leaflets. Many superb blue forms are available, such as 'Blue Jacket', 'Freedom', 'Jane Eyre' and 'Josephine'.

Height: 90cm-1·5m (3-5ft)
Spread: 60-90cm (2-3ft)
Cultivation: Well-drained moderately-fertile soils are best, in full sun or light shade. Set the plants in position in autumn or spring, and cut them down to soil-level in autumn.
Propagation: Increase named forms from 7·5-10cm (3-4in) long basal cuttings in spring, inserted in pots of sandy soil and placed in a cold frame. When the cuttings are rooted, pot them up into small pots of loam-based compost. Plant them into permanent positions in autumn or spring. when the soil is workable.

Right: **Lupinus polyphyllus 'Russell Hybrids'**
These hardy herbaceous perennials are popular and reliable plants for any garden, providing a mass of colour. They grow equally well in slightly acid or neutral soils, and in full sun or light shade.

Left: **Nemophila menziesii**
This hardy annual has a rather spreading growth habit and bears sky-blue buttercup-like flowers from early summer onwards. It is ideal for edging an annual border or even a mixed border.

Nemophila menziesii

(Nemophila insignis)
Baby Blue Eyes (UK and USA)

This bright-eyed hardy annual from California has light green deeply-cut feathery foliage and 3cm (1¼in) wide, sky-blue, flowers with white centres from early to late summer.

Lupinus polyphyllus 'Russell Hybrids' mixes with a wide range of herbaceous plants. Highlight the flowers by planting it against a dark green hedge, or use its own foliage as a backcloth for lower-growing plants.

Nemophila menziesii has flowers that are not colour dominant, so it can be mixed with plants such as the Poached Egg Plant (*Limnanthes douglasii*), with its yellow-centred white flowers.

Nicandra physaloides

Shoo-fly Plant · Apple of Peru (UK and USA)

This hardy annual from Peru is vigorous and strong growing, its spreading shoots bearing oval, mid-green leaves with finely-toothed. wavy edges. The pale-blue, bell-shaped, 4cm (1½in) wide flowers have white throats, and appear from mid to late summer. These are followed by non-edible apple-shaped green fruits that can be dried for home decoration. It is said to gain the name *physaloides* from the resemblance of the fruits to those of *Physalis alkekengi*, commonly called Chinese Lantern or Bladder Cherry.
Height: 75-90cm (2½-3ft)
Spread: 38-45cm (15-18in)
Cultivation: Rich, moist soil and a sunny position are the keys to success. When preparing the flowering position, fork in plenty of well-rotted compost.
Propagation: During late winter or early spring, sow seeds 3mm (⅛in) deep in trays of loam-based seed compost kept at 10°C (50°F). When the seedlings are large enough to handle, prick them off into seedboxes and put them in a cold frame to harden them off. Set the plants in the garden during late spring. Alternatively, sow seeds in late spring where the plants are to flower, 6mm (¼in) deep. Subsequently, thin the seedlings to 25-30cm (10-12in) apart.

Height: 18-23cm (7-9in)
Spread: 15-20cm (6-8in)
Cultivation: Although this annual grows in ordinary garden soil, it does even better in fertile, moisture-retentive soil in full sun or slight shade. Sandy soils enriched with plenty of compost are also suitable.
Propagation: During spring and early summer, sow seeds 6mm (¼in) deep in their flowering positions. When the seedlings are large enough to handle, thin them to 15cm (6in) apart. As well as being suitable for sowing in the garden, this annual can also be grown for flowering in pots in a cold greenhouse. To grow such plants, sow seeds thinly in 13cm (5in) wide pots of loam-based compost in a cold frame during late spring or early summer. When they are large enough to handle, thin the seedlings to three in each pot. Make sure the greenhouse is not kept too hot.

Right: **Nicandra physaloides**
This tall, vigorous, branching hardy annual needs space in which to develop properly. The pale-blue, bell-shaped flowers are borne over many weeks, from mid to late summer.

Nicandra physaloides gains one of its common names, Shoo-fly Plant, from its ability to repel flies. It makes a lovely choice for the back of a border, with its attractive bell-shaped flowers.

THE FLOWER BORDER

Polemonium foliosissimum

Jacob's Ladder (UK)
Jacob's Ladder · Greek Valerian (USA)

A hardy herbaceous perennial from North America, Jacob's Ladder has stiff, upright stems bearing leaves formed of narrow, dark green leaflets. From early to late summer, it bears 12mm (½in) wide mauve-blue flowers in clustered heads. The handsome flowers are highlighted by orange-yellow stamens. An early form is 'Sapphire', with light blue saucer-shaped flowers.
Height: 75-90cm (2½-3ft)
Spread: 45-60cm (1½-2ft)
Cultivation: Rich, deep, loamy soil in full sun assures success. These plants soon exhaust the soil, which will need annual mulching or feeding with fertilizer.
Propagation: The easiest way to increase this plant is by lifting and dividing established clumps in autumn or spring.

Below: **Polemonium foliosissimum**
This herbaceous perennial is ideal for any border and flowers over a long period of time. It needs rich soil, because the roots quickly exhaust the supply of nutrients.

Physostegia virginiana

(Dracocephalum virginianum)
Obedient Plant (UK)
Obedience · False Dragonhead · Lion's-head (USA)

This distinctive hardy herbaceous perennial bears long spires of mid-summer tubular pink-mauve flowers above large, glossy, dark green, coarsely-toothed leaves. The plant gets its common name from its flowers, which have hinged stalks and can be moved from side to side, remaining as positioned. Several forms are available, including 'Rose Bouquet' (pink-mauve), 'Summer Spire' (deep lilac-purple) and 'Vivid' (deep pink).
Height: 45cm-1m (1½-3½ft)
Spread: 45-60cm (1½-2ft)
Cultivation: This plant needs

Above: **Physostegia virginiana 'Rose Bouquet'**
A native of North America, this popular hardy herbaceous perennial bears spires of mauve-pink, tubular flowers which resemble small snapdragons.

ordinary fertile garden soil that does not dry out during summer. During autumn, cut it down to soil-level.
Propagation: It is easily increased by lifting and dividing plants in autumn or spring. Alternatively, during spring, take 5-7·5cm (2-3in) long cuttings, insert them in pots of sandy compost and place these in a cold frame. When the cuttings are rooted, pot them up and plant them out into their flowering positions in autumn. In cold areas with wet soil, plant them during spring.

Physostegia virginiana is a reliable plant for a mixed or herbaceous border. The deep lilac-purple variety 'Summer Spire' needs non-conflicting colours set around it at a lower level.

Polemoniums come mostly from North America, but *Polemonium caeruleum* originated in Europe and Asia as well. It gained its first name from King Polemon of Pontus, an ancient country in North-east Asia Minor.

Above: **Salvia x superba**
This hardy eye-catching herbaceous perennial forms a dominant splash of colour in any border.

Above: **Salvia viridis** *is a beautiful hardy annual with pale pink or purple flowers which feature especially striking coloured bracts at the tops of the stems. It is raised as a half-hardy or a hardy annual, and it delights in a sunny and well-drained position in the garden.*

Salvia x superba

(Salvia virgata nemorsa)
Long-branched Sage (UK)

A dominant planting of this superb hardy herbaceous perennial will immediately attract attention. Its erect stems bear abundant, rich violet-purple flower spires at their tops all summer through, so set it at the edge of a border. Dwarf forms rise to less than half the height of the type plant, and include 'Lubeca' (violet-blue, 75cm/2½ft high) and 'East Friesland' (violet-purple, 45cm/1½ft high).
Height: 45-90cm (1½-3ft)
Spread: 45-60cm (1½-2ft)
Cultivation: Rich, well-drained but moisture-retentive soil in full sun assures success. Dry soils are not suitable. Staking with twiggy pea-sticks is necessary for tall-growing forms in exposed areas. Cut down old stems to soil-level in late autumn.
Propagation: It is easily increased by lifting and dividing congested plants during autumn or spring.

Salvia viridis

(Salvia horminum)

This hardy annual from Southern Europe bears 12mm (½in) long pale pink or purple flowers from mid to late summer. It is better known, however, for its 4cm (1½in) long brightly coloured terminal bracts (modified leaves), which can be dried with the stems for home decoration. There are several fine forms, with a range of coloured bracts, such as 'Blue Bouquet' (rich purple-blue bracts) and 'Rose Bouquet' (rose-carmine bracts).
Height: 38-45cm (15-18in)
Spread: 23-30cm (9-12in)
Cultivation: Ordinary well-drained soil in full sun suits it. To encourage well-branched plants, pinch out the growing tips when the plants are only a few inches high.
Propagation: During late spring or early summer, sow seeds 6mm (¼in) deep where the plants are to flower. When the seedlings are large enough to handle, thin them out to 23cm (9in) apart. You can raise earlier-flowering plants by sowing seeds thinly in trays of loam-based compost at 18°C (64°F) during late winter or early spring. When the seedlings are large enough to handle, prick them off into pots of loam-based compost and place them in a cold frame to harden off.

Salvia x superba demands space to be at its best. Plant it at the front of the border, with tall light blue delphiniums at the back and a sandwich of yellow achillea between them.

Salvia viridis, better known as *Salvia horminum*, is best used to create dominant colour at the tops of its stems. It is more often grown for its coloured bracts than for its flowers.

THE FLOWER BORDER

Above: **Trachymene caerulea**
The delicate heads of small lavender-blue flowers appear from mid-summer to autumn. This is a useful plant for bringing delicate blue shades to flower arrangements.

Above: **Tradescantia virginiana 'Isis'**
This well-known Spiderwort has striking purple-blue flowers during most of summer. Well-drained but moisture-retentive soil ensures success with this reliable plant.

Right: **Tulip 'Lilac Time'**
This beautiful tulip from Division 7 is distinctive, with its mauve, lily-like flowers. Flowers in this division are usually 15-20cm (6-8in) wide and appear in mid-spring.

Trachymene caerulea

(Didiscus caeruleus)
Blue Lace Flower · Queen Anne's Lace (UK)
Blue Lace Flower (USA)

This is one of the most delicate and pretty of all half-hardy annuals. It forms a bushy plant with light green, deeply-divided foliage. The small, dainty, lavender-blue flowers are displayed in heads 2·5-5cm (1-2in) wide and appear from mid-summer to autumn. They are suitable for cutting for home decoration, but the leaves and stems are sticky to touch.
Height: 45cm (1½ft)
Spread: 25-30cm (10-12in)
Cultivation: Ordinary well-cultivated garden soil and a sunny, sheltered position suit it.
Propagation: During late winter and early spring, sow seeds 3mm (⅛in) deep in trays of loam-based seed compost at 16°C (61°F). When the seedlings are large enough to handle, prick them out into small pots or boxes of seed compost. Plant the young plants out into the garden as soon as all risk of frost has passed.

Tradescantia virginiana

Spiderwort · Trinity Flower (UK)
Common Spiderwort · Widow's Tears (USA)

This hardy herbaceous perennial, with smooth, glossy, strap-like, dull-green leaves and long lasting, 2·5-4cm (1-1½in) wide, three-petalled flowers, is a delight throughout summer and into autumn. It is the hybrids from *T. virginiana* or *T. x andersoniana* that are mainly grown. Some botanical authorities suggest these hybrids are derived from the former species, while other botanists name the latter as a parent. Whatever their origin, the resulting plants are superb and include 'Carmine Glow' (carmine), 'Isis' (purple-blue), 'Iris Pritchard' (white, stained azure blue) and 'Purewell Giant' (carmine-purple).
Height: 45-60cm (1½-2ft)
Spread: 45cm (1½ft)
Cultivation: Ordinary garden soil, well-drained but also moisture-retentive, is best. In late autumn, cut the plants down to soil-level.
Propagation: Lift and divide congested clumps in spring.

Tulips

The range of form and colour of these well-known hardy bulbs is as wide as their possible uses in the garden. They can be used in bedding schemes during spring, in mixed borders or rock gardens, and in tubs or troughs for brightening up a patio in spring. There is a wide range of species, and in addition botanists have classified those that have been created by bulb experts into fifteen divisions, encompassing the wide range of flower sizes, shapes and heights. These are:
Division 1—Single Early (15-38cm/6-15in): The single flowers appear in spring when grown out-of-doors, or during winter indoors. Each flower is 7·5-13cm (3-5in) wide and sometimes opens flat when in direct and full sun. Many purple varieties are available, as well as ones with white, pink, red, orange and yellow flowers.
Division 2—Double Early (30-38cm/12-15in): The double flowers appear in spring when grown out-of-doors in bedding schemes, or earlier when forced indoors.

Trachymene caerulea from Australia soon attracts attention when grown in a dominant drift among hardy annuals or in a mixed border. It can also be grown in pots in an unheated greenhouse for summer colour.

Tradescantia virginiana and **T. x andersoniana** are ideal for a mixed or herbaceous border. Many plants combine well with them, including border geraniums and *Campanula lactiflora* 'Pritchard's Blue'.

Division 10—Parrot (45-60cm/ 1½-2ft): These bear flowers up to 20cm (8in) wide in mid-spring, easily recognizable by their feather-like, heavily-fringed petals. The colour range includes brilliant white, pink, orange and yellow, as well as some lovely purples.

Division 11—Double Late (45-60cm/1½-2ft): These have very large and showy double flowers, similar to paeonies and up to 20cm (8in) wide. They remain in flower for a long period during mid-spring. There are some stunning violet varieties, as well as white, orange, pink, red and yellow ones. There are also multi-coloured forms, with stripes and edgings.

Division 12—Kaufmanniana varieties (10-25cm/4-10in): These have been developed from *Tulipa kaufmanniana*, and have fine-pointed flowers that open nearly flat, giving the appearance of water-lilies. They appear in spring on sturdy stems and are ideal for fronts of borders, rock gardens and containers. Most have two-coloured flowers.

Division 13—Fosteriana varieties (45cm/1½in): These are derived from *Tulipa fosteriana* and display large blunt-ended flowers in reds and yellows in mid-spring.

Division 14—Greigii varieties (25cm/10in): These are mainly derived from *Tulipa greigii*, and produce brilliant red, yellow and near-white long-lasting flowers during mid-spring.

Cultivation: When growing tulips in the garden, select well-drained soil, preferably facing south and in a sheltered position. Plant the bulbs 15cm (6in) deep during early winter, spacing them 10-15cm (4-6in) apart. Remove dead flowers and dig up the bulbs when the leaves turn yellow. However, if the bed is needed earlier, dig up the bulbs as soon as flowering is over and heel them into a trench until the foliage has yellowed and died down.

Propagation: The easiest way is to remove the bulb offsets clustered at the bases of the bulbs. Plant these in a nursery bed and leave them to develop into flowering-sized bulbs.

Each flower is 10cm (4in) wide and rather like a double paeony. The colour range is wide, including good purple varieties, as well as red, violet, pink and yellow ones.

Division 3—Mendel (38-50cm/ 15-20in): These flower later than the previous types, with rounded 10-13cm (4-5in) wide blooms on somewhat slender stems. Colours include white and red, as well as yellow. They look like a cross between single early types and Darwins.

Division 4—Triumph (up to 50cm/ 20in): In mid-spring, these bear angular-looking 10-13cm (4-5in) wide flowers on strong stems. There are lovely lilac-flowered varieties, as well as red and pink ones.

Division 5—Darwin Hybrids (60-75cm/2-2½ft): These have some of the largest and most brilliant flowers, up to 18cm (7in) wide; they appear during mid-spring. There are multi-coloured forms, as well as purple, red, orange and yellow varieties.

Division 6—Darwin (60-75cm/ 2-2½ft): These are extensively used in bedding schemes, producing rounded flowers up to 13cm (5in) wide in late spring. There are some excellent purple varieties, also yellow, white, pink and red ones.

Division 7—Lily-flowered (45-60cm/1½-2ft): These are character-ized by the narrow waists of their flowers, also by the pointed petals that curl outwards as much as 20cm (8in) during mid-spring. They look especially attractive when massed in bedding schemes. Colours include white, orange, red, yellow and multi-colours.

Division 8—Cottage (up to 90cm/ 3ft): This old grouping has oval or rounded flowers 10-13cm (4-5in) wide in mid-spring. The petals sometimes have a hint of fringing, and are looser than those of other varieties. As well as lilac, flower colours include green, white, pink, red and yellow.

Division 9—Rembrandt (75cm/ 2½ft): These tulips all have 'broken' colours. The rounded 13cm (5in) wide flowers display vivid splashes of colour on the petals during mid-spring. Base colours include violet, as well as brown, white, orange, red, yellow and pink.

For a **blue and gold display**, try the dark blue Darwin tulip (Division 6) 'La Tulipe Noire' with the orange Siberian Wallflower *Cheiranthus* x *allionii* 'Golden Bedder'. For extra shades of blue, add a few Forget-me-nots (*Myosotis*).

For a **mixture of creamy-white and blue**, try planting a bed with the mauve-blue Parrot tulip (Division 10) 'Blue Parrot', dark purple Darwin tulip (Division 6) 'Queen of Night' and the Wallflower 'Ivory White'.

THE FLOWER BORDER

Right: **Veronica prostrata**
*This beautiful ground-covering
veronica produces masses of small
deep blue flowers from early to
mid-summer. There are several
superb forms, including a very
low-growing type.*

Veronica prostrata

(Veronica rupestris · V. teucrium
prostrata)

A hardy mat-forming alpine veronica,
this is a distant form of the
Hungarian, or Saw-leaved, Speedwell
from Southern Europe and Northern
Asia. It is useful as a ground cover
plant, displaying toothed mid-green
leaves and 5-7·5cm (2-3in) long
spikes of deep blue flowers from
early to mid-summer. Several reliable
forms are available, including
'Spode Blue' (clear pale blue),
'Rosea' (deep pink), 'Alba' (white)
and a dwarf form 'Pygmaea' (5cm/
2in high, with deep blue flowers).
Height: 10-20cm (4-8in)
Spread: 38-45cm (15-18in)
Cultivation: Any well-drained garden
soil and a sunny position suit it.
Propagation: During mid-summer,
take 5cm (2in) long cuttings and
insert them in pots of equal parts
peat and sharp sand. Place the pots
in a cold frame and when the
cuttings are rooted, pot them up
singly into loam-based compost.
During the following spring, plant
them out into the garden.

Veronica spicata

Spiked Speedwell (UK)

An upright slim-flowered hardy
herbaceous perennial, this veronica
is well-suited to the front of a border.
It displays long, toothed, lance-
shaped, mid-green leaves. The
narrow, 7·5-15cm (3-6in) long spires
of small blue flowers are borne
throughout mid-summer. Several
superb forms are worth growing,
including 'Blue Fox' (ultramarine
blue) and 'Barcarolle' (rose-pink).
Veronica longifolia is another
purple-blue-flowered border plant.
It rises up to 1·2m (4ft) and bears
15cm (6in) long terminal spires of

flowers from early to late summer.
To create a dominant clump, set the
individual plants about 45cm (1½ft)
apart. *Veronica virginica* is another
good border species, with pale
blue spires of flowers.
Height: 30-45cm (1-1½ft)
Spread: 30-38cm (12-15in)
Cultivation: Well-drained but
moisture-retentive friable soil in full
sun or slight shade assures success.
In late autumn, cut the stems down
to soil-level.
Propagation: During spring, lift and
divide congested clumps—you can
usually do this every three or four
years. This ensures healthy plants.

Top right: **Veronica spicata**
*This is a reliable hardy herbaceous
perennial for the front of a border,
where it can display its spires of
small blue flowers to advantage
during mid-summer. There are
several excellent varieties from
which to choose.*

Right: **Catananche caerulea**
*This beautiful short-lived perennial
brings a wealth of colour to a border.
It is also excellent as a cut-flower,
and can be dried for winter decoration in the home. The flowers appear
during summer. For details see
under* **Further plants to consider**
on the opposite page.

Veronica prostrata blends well in a rock garden with
yellow-flowered plants such as *Linum flavum*, with
2·5cm (1in) wide mid-summer flowers, and the
ever-reliable *Hypericum olympicum*, with
golden-yellow flowers.

Further plants to consider

Ajuga reptans
Bugle (UK) · Carpet Bugleweed (USA)
Height: 10-25cm (4-10in)   Spread: 30-50cm (12-20in)
A well-known, soil-smothering, hardy herbaceous perennial, with whorls or blue flowers borne on upright stems during mid-summer. The form 'Atropurpurea' is distinctive, with purple leaves.

Campanula persicifolia 'Telham Beauty'
Peach-leaved Campanula (UK) · Peach-bells · Willow Bellflower (USA)
Height: 60-90cm (2-3ft)   Spread: 30-38cm (12-15in)
A delightful perennial, with an evergreen basal rosette. The rich blue, 2·5cm (1in) wide, saucer-shaped flowers appear during mid-summer. 'Pride of Exmouth' displays rich lavender-blue flowers.

Catananche caerulea
Cupid's Dart (UK and USA)
Height: 45-75cm (1½-2½ft)   Spread: 45-60cm (1½-2ft)
A short-lived herbaceous perennial with narrow, lance-shaped leaves and lavender-blue flowers during summer. The form 'Major' bears richer blue flowers.

Delphinium elatum
Height: 90cm-1·5m (3-5ft)   Spread: 45-60cm (1½-2ft)
The actual species is seldom grown, but it is the well-known *Belladonna* and *Elatum* (also known as 'large-flowered') types that are widely grown. The range of blue-flowered forms is wide, including 'Blue Tit' (indigo-blue), 'Blue Jade' (sky-blue), 'Page Boy' (brilliant mid-blue), 'Blue Bees' (bright pale blue), 'Bonita' (gentian-blue), 'Wendy' (gentian-blue, flecked purple), 'Cressida' (pale blue with a white eye) and 'Mullion' (cobalt-blue with a dark eye).

Geranium x magnificum
(Geranium ibericum · Geranium platypetalum)
Height: 45-60cm (1½-2ft)   Spread: 45-50cm (18-20in)
An eye-catching hybrid geranium, with violet-blue 2·5cm (1in) wide flowers during mid to late summer.

Geranium pratense 'Johnson's Blue'
Height: 38cm (15in)   Spread: 38-45cm (15-18in)
A well-known light-blue mid-summer flowering hardy herbaceous perennial. The flowers are borne amongst mid-green five or seven-lobed leaves.

Limonium latifolium
Sea Lavender · Statice (UK)
Height: 60cm (2ft)   Spread: 45-60cm (1½-2ft)
A distinctive hardy perennial, formerly classified as *Statice*. From mid-to late summer, it displays lavender-blue flowers in large, loose heads. Two good forms are 'Violetta' (violet) and 'Blue Cloud' (lavender-blue).

Veronica spicata is a British native plant that gains its second name from the spike-like arrangement of its flowers. The related *V. beccabunga* acquired its unusual name from the old word *beck*, 'a rill or ditch', and *bung*, 'a purse'.

CHAPTER TWO

ROCK AND NATURALIZED GARDENS

There is a wealth of blue, mauve and violet-coloured plants for the rock garden or naturalized site. Many are of a bulbous nature, and produce corms, rhizomes or true bulbs. These include Autumn Crocus, *Colchicum autumnale*, which, together with *Colchicum speciosum*, brings splashes of colour in autumn. *Crocus tomasinianus* and Glory of the Snow, *Chionodoxa luciliae*, flower in late winter and early spring. Then there is a wide range of irises. Varieties such as Japanese Iris, *Iris kaempferi*, the crested *Iris gracilipes* and the diminutive *Iris reticulata* are a joy on their own. Grape Hyacinth *Muscari armeniacum*, *Scilla tubergeniana* and *Scilla sibirica* are further candidates, while the Spanish Bluebell, *Endymion hispanicus*, a dominant and widely-grown bulbous plant that at one time seemed to change its name every time a botanist sneezed, is wonderful for creating blanket colour in moist, fertile and slightly shaded areas.

Garden pools and their edges can support a wide range of blue-flowered plants. Those for planting in water include Pickerel Plant, *Pontederia cordata*, Floating Water Hyacinth, *Eichhornia crassipes*, with spikes of lavender-blue flowers, and Water Forget-me-not, *Myosotis palustris*, with pale blue yellow-eyed flowers from spring to mid-summer. The Water Forget-me-not is suitable for water up to 7·5cm (3in) deep, while the Floating Water Hyacinth survives deeper water but displays its flowers above the surface. Primulas, *Iris kaempferi*, *Iris sibirica* and meconopsis prefer the moist conditions around a pool, but not a swamp.

Lithodora diffusa, better known as *Lithospermum diffusum*, is one of the best blue-flowered perennials for a rock garden, with its charming funnel-shaped flowers. 'Grace Ward', with intense blue flowers, is one of the most familiar forms. *Edraianthus pumilio* is another plant with funnel-shaped flowers that makes a good choice for a rock garden.

Left: **Grape Hyacinths (Muscari armeniacum)**, *with their tightly-clustered azure-blue flower heads, create a strong colour contrast with a mixed assortment of yellow, pink and red polyanthus.*

ROCK AND NATURALIZED GARDENS

Anemone blanda

Blue Windflower (UK)
Windflower (USA)

This welcome and reliable spring-flowering plant has rather fern-like deeply-cut dark green leaves and 2·5-4cm (1-1½in) wide daisy-like flowers in pale blue, pink, lavender or white.

Height: 13-15cm (5-6in)
Spread: 10-13cm (4-5in)
Cultivation: Well-drained fertile soil, neutral or slighty acid, in light dappled shade, suits it best. The corms are best planted in autumn, 5cm (2in) deep and 13-15cm (5-6in) apart.
Propagation: Lift and divide congested clumps in late summer. Alternatively, sow seeds when ripe in pots or boxes of loam-based compost, placing them in a cold frame. Prick off the seedlings into boxes when they are large enough to handle.

Right: **Anemone blanda 'Blue Pearl'**
Anemones are always welcome in spring, with their neat, daisy-like flowers with bright centres. There is a range of colours, including this striking blue variety. They can be naturalized beneath trees or set in neat clumps in a rock garden.

Aubrieta deltoidea

This is one of the best-known rock garden plants, well suited for covering large areas and for trailing over walls. It is also useful as an edging to paths and for combining with herbaceous plants. There are many forms, originated from selected seedlings of this hardy, spreading and low-growing evergreen perennial. These include 'Barker's Double' (rose-purple), 'Dr. Mules' (violet-purple), 'Henslow Purple' (bright purple), 'Triumphant' (blue) and 'Tauricola' (deep purple-blue).

Height: 7·5-10cm (3-4in)
Spread: 45-60cm (1½-2ft)
Cultivation: Well-drained, slightly limy garden soil and a sunny position suit it best. Keep the plants neat by trimming them after flowering.
Propagation: The plants can be easily increased by lifting and dividing them during early autumn.

Far right: **Aubrieta deltoidea 'Ballawley Amethyst'**
This handsome, spreading and trailing evergreen perennial is ideal for cascading over walls, as an edging to paths and even for growing with herbaceous plants. There are many forms to choose from, with colours ranging from pink through to blue and violet-blue.

Right: **Anemone coronaria**
This is the well-known florist's anemone, popular in both borders and in rock gardens, as well as being extensively grown for cut-flowers.

Anemone blanda is striking when naturalized among the dappled light filtering through silver-barked trees. Also, try a mixture of anemones, polyanthus, Grape Hyacinths and Drumstick Primulas.

Aubrietia deltoidea harmonizes with many others, including the hardy pink or white perennial *Arabis caucasica*, the yellow-flowered bulb *Tulipa tarda*, and the hardy perennial yellow *Alyssum saxatile*.

Above: **Campanula cochleariifolia**
*This hardy dwarf perennial with its
nodding thimble-like flowers is a
delight in a rock garden. It is one of
the most amenable and rewarding
of all campanulas.*

Campanula cochleariifolia

(Campanula pusilla)
Fairies' Thimbles (UK)

A dainty, undemanding easily-grown
hardy dwarf perennial, this is ideal
for a rock garden. It displays
mid-green, shallow-toothed leaves
and 12mm (½in) long, nodding,
bell-shaped, sky-blue flowers during
mid to late summer. A white form is
also available.

Height: 10-15cm (4-6in)
Spread: 30-38cm (12-15in)
Cultivation: Well-drained soil and
full sun suit it. Set the plants in
position in autumn or spring.
Propagation: It is easily increased by
lifting and dividing large clumps in
autumn or spring. Alternatively, take
soft cuttings 5cm (2in) long in
spring, insert them in pots of equal
parts peat and sharp sand and place
these in a cold frame. When the
cuttings are rooted, pot them up into
small pots until they are large
enough to be planted in the garden.
When given thoroughly drained soil,
it soon spreads to form large
mats of flowers and foliage.

Campanula cochleariifolia is ideal for trailing and
cascading over rocks. It also delights in growing
between natural stone paving slabs, and is superb
for planting at the sides of paths in large rock gardens.

ROCK AND NATURALIZED GARDENS

Above: **Chionodoxa luciliae gigantea**
The dominant colour of these delicate flowers will brighten any garden in late winter. It is not a fussy plant, and grows well in any well-drained soil in full sun. All chionodoxas are superb for bringing colour during late winter.

Chionodoxa luciliae

Glory of the Snow (UK and USA)

This bright hardy bulb from Asia Minor produces brilliant sky-blue, 2·5cm (1in) wide flowers during late winter and early spring. Each flower has a white centre. The form *Chionodoxa luciliae gigantea*, often called *C. gigantea*, is larger, and has pale violet-blue 4cm (1½in) wide flowers with small white centres. Chionodoxas are ideal for rock gardens, for naturalizing in short, fine grass, and for placing at the front of borders.
Height: 18-20cm (7-8in)
Spread: 7·5-10cm (3-4in)
Cultivation: Ordinary well-drained garden soil and full sun assure success. Plant the bulbs 6·5cm (2½in) deep.
Propagation: Lift and divide large clumps as soon as the leaves have died down. Replant the bulbs immediately.

Colchicum autumnale

Autumn Crocus (UK)
Autumn Crocus · Fall Crocus · Meadow Saffron · Mysteria · Wonder Bulb (USA)

This hardy corm-bearing plant bears large mid to dark green leaves up to 25cm (10in) long in spring and early summer, which later die back. In autumn, it produces 15cm (6in) high, goblet-shaped, rosy-lilac flowers, often with a chequered pattern. There are also some lovely purplish forms, as well as white varieties and 'Roseum-plenum', with double rose-pink flowers.
Height: 25-30cm (10-12in)
Spread: 20-25cm (8-10in)
Cultivation: It delights in well-drained soil in full sun or light shade. Plant the corms during autumn, 7·5cm (3in) deep in small groups.
Propagation: It can be raised from seed, but the production of flowering-sized corms takes up to seven years.

Above: **Colchicum speciosum**
This unusual corm-bearing plant flowers in autumn after its foliage has died down. It thrives in sun or partial shade and is superb for bringing colour to the garden.

It is easier to lift congested clumps when the leaves have died down and remove the offsets. Plant them out in a nursery bed for a couple of years until ready for their final positions, and replant the parent corms, too.

Colchicum speciosum

Autumn Crocus (UK)

This distinctive hardy corm-bearing plant from Asia Minor displays 30cm (1ft) long, 10cm (4in) wide leaves in spring and early summer. In autumn, when the leaves have died back, its 15cm (6in) high stems bear flowers in a wide range of colours, from white to pinkish-lilac

---

Chionodoxa luciliae is superb for planting under the golden-yellow flowers of the Chinese Witch Hazel (*Hamamelis mollis*). It also blends perfectly with *Narcissus cyclamineus* 'February Gold'.

Colchicum autumnale, the Autumn Crocus or Meadow Saffron, has nothing to do with crocuses or with saffron, which comes from *Crocus sativus*. However, its dried corms are a valuable ingredient of medicines.

and reddish-purple. It has been
crossed with other species to create
many superb hybrids.
Height: 30-38cm (12-15in)
Spread: 25-30cm (10-12in)
Cultivation: Well-drained soil in full
sun or light shade suits it. During
autumn, plant the corms 7·5-10cm
(3-4in) deep in small clumps.
Propagation: It can be raised from
seed, but the production of flowering-
sized corms takes up to seven years.
It is easier to lift congested clumps
when the leaves have died down
and remove the offsets, planting
them out in a nursery bed for a
couple of years until ready for their
final positions. Replant the large,
parent corms, too.

Colchicum speciosum is useful for planting under
shrubs and trees, where its spring and early
summer leaves cannot swamp nearby plants. It is
superb for planting under species roses.

ROCK AND NATURALIZED GARDENS

Convolvulus sabatius

(Convolvulus mauritanicus)

This handsome North American trailing and mat-forming perennial is not fully hardy, so it is ideal for warm, sunny rock gardens or even in hanging-baskets. The 2·5-4cm (1-1½in) long, almost round, mid-green leaves are surmounted by 2·5cm (1in) wide, purple-blue, trumpet-shaped flowers with small white throats borne singly from mid to late summer.

Height: 5-7·5cm (2-3in)
Spread: 45-60cm (1½-2ft)
Cultivation: Light, well-drained, sandy soil in a warm area and a sheltered position suit it best. It is only really successful in warmer areas.
Propagation: During mid-summer, take 5cm (2in) long cuttings, inserting them in pots of equal parts peat and sharp sand, placing these in a cold frame. When the cuttings are rooted, pot them up singly into small pots of loam-based compost and over-winter them in a frost-proof greenhouse. Wait until late spring before planting them out into the garden or in containers.

Below: **Convolvulus sabatius**
This delightful member of the bindweed family is often better known as Convolvulus mauritanicus. *It is not fully hardy, but well worth growing for its beautiful blue flowers from mid-summer onwards.*

Above: **Crocus tomasinianus**
This is one of the earliest crocuses to flower, in late winter. It needs protection from cold winds but, once established, it will thrive in most gardens.

Crocus tomasinianus

An attractive late-winter flowering bulb, this crocus displays narrow dark green leaves with pronounced white midribs. The flowers range in colour from pale lavender to reddish-purple and are borne during late winter and into early spring. Good varieties include 'Barr's Purple' and 'Whitewell Purple', both purple.

Convolvulus sabatius can be used in a rock garden to cover large, bare areas or to trail over rocks where it helps to fuse the various elements of the rock garden together.

Crocus tomasinianus mixes well with many other late-winter flowering plants, such as *Cyclamen coum* and the Winter Aconite (*Eranthis hyemalis*) or with early-flowering shrubs like *Mahonia japonica*.

Crocus vernus

(Crocus neapolitanus)
Dutch Crocus (UK and USA)

The species is the parent of the many varieties of Dutch Crocus with large goblet-shaped flowers in a range of colours including lilac, purple and white, often with striking veining. Flowering is during early spring. There are many varieties to choose from and blue or purple ones include 'Queen of the Blues' (lavender-blue), 'Striped Beauty' (dark purple-blue stripes on a silver-white background and with a violet-purple base to the petals) and 'Purpureus Grandiflorus' (purple-blue).

Height: 7·5-13cm (3-5in)
Spread: 4-5cm (1½-2in)
Cultivation: Well-drained soil and a sheltered and sunny position suit it. It can be grown in rock gardens or naturalized in the short, fine grass of an alpine meadow.
Propagation: Lift and divide the corms when the foliage has died down after flowering. Remove the small cormlets and replant them.

Below: **Crocus vernus 'Striped Beauty'**
This Dutch crocus has delicate veining on its large, goblet-shaped flowers. The bulbs increase naturally until large drifts are formed if given free-draining soil and a positon where it gets plenty of sun.

Height: 7·5-10cm (3-4in)
Spread: 5-6·5cm (2-2½in)
Cultivation: Ordinary well-drained soil and a sunny, sheltered place free from cold winds are suitable. It is often recommended for naturalizing in short grass, but it does not always do well in such a position and is best planted in the bare soil of rock gardens or under deciduous trees and shrubs. Set the corms 6·5-7·5cm (2½-3in) deep.
Propagation: It will seed and naturalize itself quite readily, especially in bare soil. Alternatively, remove cormlets from around the corms. When replanted, these take two or three years to produce good plants.

Crocus vernus is a perfect match for *Narcissus cyclamineus* 'February Gold', with bright yellow spring flowers, and *Crocus aureus* 'Dutch Gold' which has deep yellow blooms.

ROCK AND NATURALIZED GARDENS

Left: **Cyclamen hederifolium**
This is one of the hardiest and most free-flowering of all cyclamens for creating colour in the garden. The flowers appear from late summer to early winter, growing best under trees where the plant gains shelter and shade.

Edraianthus pumilio

Grassy Bells (USA)

This hardy herbaceous perennial from Yugoslavia is an excellent rock garden plant. It produces clumps of narrow grey-green leaves, and clusters of upturned lavender-blue funnel-shaped flowers during early summer. It is ideal for planting in troughs and stone sinks.
Height: 5-7·5cm (2-3in)
Spread: 15-25cm (6-10in)

Cultivation: Well-drained deep soil and a sunny position suit it best.
Propagation: During late winter, sow seeds in small pots of loam-based seed compost and place them in a cold frame. Prick out the seedlings into bigger pots when they are large enough to handle. Alternatively, in late summer, take 5cm (2in) long cuttings and insert them in pots of equal parts peat and sharp sand, placing them in a cold frame. When they are rooted, pot up the cuttings. Plant them in the garden in spring.

Below: **Edraianthus pumilio**
This is an excellent choice for a well-drained scree bed in a rock garden, or for a trough or stone sink. The lavender-blue, funnel-shaped flowers appear in early summer.

Cyclamen hederifolium

(Cyclamen neapolitanum)
Baby Cyclamen (USA)

An easily-grown, long-lived, free-flowering and extremely hardy corm-bearing plant, this cyclamen has deep green leaves, red beneath and with silvery markings above. The variable, mauve to pink, 2·5cm (1in) long flowers appear from late summer to early winter. There is also a white form.
Height: 10cm (4in)
Spread: 10-15cm (4-6in)
Cultivation: Humus-rich, well-drained soil in light, dappled shade suits it best. Plant the corms in late summer, where they can be left undisturbed for many years. It is a long-lived plant and even old corms produce flowers.
Propagation: The corms do not produce offsets, so they must be increased by sowing seeds in late summer, thinly and in pots of loam-based compost. Place the pots in a cold frame or against a wall. When the seedlings are large enough to handle, prick them off into individual pots of a loam-based compost. Do this as soon as their second leaves appear. When they are strong and well-grown, plant them into their final positions.

Cyclamen hederifolium is ideal for naturalizing in bare soil beneath trees, planting on banks, or in a rock garden. If left undisturbed, the plants eventually create large drifts of colour.

Edraianthus pumilio is ideal for a scree bed, where its foliage blends with small stone chippings. Even when grown in a stone sink, it can be given a similar background.

Endymion hispanicus

(Scilla campanulata · Scilla hispanica)
Spanish Bluebell (UK)
Spanish Bluebell · Spanish Jacinth ·
Bell-flowered Squill (USA)

A dominating plant, this bluebell has broad strap-like leaves and blue, pink or white bell-shaped flowers, suspended from upright stems, which appear from spring to mid-summer. Several varieties are available, including 'Excelsior' (deep blue) and 'Myosotis' (clear blue).
Height: 30cm (1ft)
Spread: 15-30cm (6-8in)
Cultivation: Fertile, moist but not boggy soil and an open or slightly shaded position are best. It is most suited to a moist wild garden.
Propagation: Self-sown seedlings appear if the seeds are allowed to fall on surrounding soil. Alternatively, lift and divide clumps annually, replanting them immediately as the bulbs do not have outer skins and soon become dry and damaged. The bulbs do not store well, shrivelling if kept too dry.

Right: **Erythronium dens-canis**
This is a beautiful corm-bearing plant for a moist naturalized garden or the side of an informal pool. It needs shade and a north-facing slope, which help to prevent the soil drying out during summer.

Below: **Endymion hispanicus**
This striking bluebell forms large clumps in moist soil under light shade. When set in light woodland in a wild garden, it creates a carpet of colour from spring to mid-summer.

Erythronium dens-canis

Dog's-tooth Violet (UK and USA)

This hardy corm-bearing plant for wild gardens has broad lance-shaped leaves blotched with brown or grey. During spring, it displays pink-purple nodding six-petalled 5-7·5cm (2-3in) wide flowers with reflexed petals, resembling those of the Turk's Cap Lily, *Lilium martagon*. Several forms are available, including 'Lilac Wonder' (pale purple) and 'Purple King' (rich purple). White and pink forms are also available.
Height: 15cm (6in)
Spread: 10-15cm (4-6in)
Cultivation: Moisture-retentive but not totally saturated soil is needed. Semi-shade and a north-facing slope are desirable. Set the corms in position in late summer, where they can be left undisturbed for several years to produce a lovely display.
Propagation: The quickest way to increase this plant is by removing offsets in late summer, when the leaves have died down. Place them in a nursery bed for three or four years to develop into plants large enough to be set in the garden. Growing from seed takes five or more years to produce sizeable plants. During this period, keep the nursery bed free from weeds and well watered.

Endymion hispanicus can be planted with a wide range of plants, such as polyanthus, or underneath *Magnolia* x *soulangiana* with its white chalice-shaped flowers in spring. It also looks good with other bulbous flowers.

Erythroniums are a delight in a moist, naturalized area. Other species useful for creating colour contrast are the American Trout Lily (*E. revolutum*), with pink flowers, and *E. tuolumnense*, with bright yellow flowers.

ROCK AND NATURALIZED GARDENS

Gentiana acaulis

(Gentiana kochiana · G. alpina · G. clusii)
Trumpet Gentian (UK)
Stemless Gentian (USA)

This is a beautiful hardy perennial for a rock garden, creating early summer colour. The brilliant blue, 5-7·5cm (2-3in) long, trumpet-shaped flowers are near stemless and borne amid mats of glossy, mid-green leaves.
Height: 7·5cm (3in)
Spread: 38-45cm (15-18in)
Cultivation: Heavy, gritty, moisture-retentive but well-drained loam and a sunny position suit it. Set the plants in position during spring.
Propagation: It is easily increased by division of the plants in late spring or early summer. Alternatively, take 5cm (2in) long cuttings from basal shoots in mid to late spring. Insert them in pots of equal parts peat and sharp sand and place these in a cold frame. Pot up the cuttings, when rooted, into small pots of loam-based compost and replace in the cold frame. Plant out into the garden during spring of the following year.

Right: **Gentiana acaulis**
A beautiful but often variable plant for a rock garden, this gentian displays its brilliant blue trumpets in early summer. It often spreads to form a large clump only a few inches high.

Gentiana septemfida

Crested Gentian (USA)

This hardy, reliable and undemanding gentian from Iran and Asia Minor has lance-shaped, mid-green leaves and a profusion of terminal, deep blue flowers from mid to late summer. Each flower is about 4cm (1½in) long and resembles an upturned trumpet.
Height: 20-30cm (8-12in)
Spread: 25-30cm (10-12in)
Cultivation: Any good, rich, moisture-retentive garden soil suits it. Grow it in either full sun or light shade. Fortunately, it is one of the easiest gentians to grow.

Propagation: Good forms are best raised from 5cm (2in) long cuttings taken in spring and inserted in pots of equal parts peat and sharp sand, placed in a cold frame. When the cuttings are rooted, pot them up into small pots and replace in the cold frame until spring of the following year. It can also be increased by sowing seeds in autumn and placing them in a cold frame.

Right: **Gentiana septemfida**
This is one of the easiest gentians to grow, with an abundance of deep blue upturned trumpet-like flowers from mid to late summer. It is ideal for nestling in a rock garden.

Gentiana acaulis blends with several other rock garden plants, including saxifragas, *Violas cornuta*, the Pasque Flower (*Pulsatilla vulgaris*), *Aster alpinus*, *Thymus drucei* and *Geranium dalmaticum*.

Gentiana septemfida is superb on its own in a rock-garden pocket, but also combines well with alpine species of gypsophila, such as *Gypsophila cerastioides* and *G. repens*, both with white or pink flowers.

Gentiana sino-ornata

This is an outstanding autumn-flowering gentian with 5cm (2in) long, brilliant blue, trumpet-shaped flowers. These are striped with a deeper blue, as well as greenish-yellow. The leaves are narrow, mid-green and rather grass-like, producing a pleasant backcloth for the flowers. This beautiful gentian was discovered by the world-famous plant hunter George Forrest (1873-1932) in 1910-11 in South-west China. On the same expedition Forrest collected seeds of the beautiful shrub *Pieris formosa forrestii*, which was named in his honour.

Height: 15cm (6in)
Spread: 30-34cm (12-18in)
Cultivation: Fertile, deep, peaty acid soil and a shaded position suit it best. Take care that the soil does not dry out during hot summers. Set the plants out in the garden during spring when the soil is warm.
Propagation: The easiest way to increase this plant is by lifting and dividing large clumps in spring.

Ipheion uniflorum

(Brodiaea uniflora · Milla uniflora · Triteleia uniflora)
Spring Starflower (UK and USA)

This beautiful and reliable bulbous plant forms a hummock of grass-like leaves and 5cm (2in) wide, six-petalled, star-shaped, scented flowers during spring. They range from white to deep lavender-blue in colour. There are several good varieties, including 'Caeruleum' (pale blue), 'Wisley Blue' (violet-blue) and 'Violaceum' (violet).

Height: 15-20cm (6-8in)
Spread: 7·5-10cm (3-4in), but plants grow together to form a large clump.
Cultivation: Ordinary well-drained garden soil in full sun suits it. A sheltered position is also needed. Plant the bulbs 5cm (2in) deep in autumn.
Propagation: During autumn, lift and divide large clumps, replanting the bulbs immediately so that they do not dry out. You can also do this immediately after flowering.

Right: **Gentiana sino-ornata**
This beautiful and well-known Chinese and Tibetan gentian is a true delight in autumn, and when seen in a large drift is highly memorable. It needs a soil rich in leafmould. The narrow mid-green leaves provide a perfect foil for the dominantly-coloured, brilliant blue, trumpet-shaped flowers.

Below: **Ipheion uniflorum 'Violaceum'**
This beautiful form of the Spring Starflower bears lovely six-petalled flowers during spring. It is native to Peru and Argentina. It is ideal for creating low hummocks of colour alongside paths, and looks especially attractive at the sides of crazy-paving and gravel paths.

Gentiana sino-ornata is often difficult to combine with other plants, and is therefore best seen on its own, planted as a large, bold splash of colour against a wall or foliage plants.

Iphelon uniflorum makes a welcome early splash of colour in rock gardens or as an edging to paths. In borders it can be combined with deciduous azaleas and *Rhododendron luteum.*

ROCK AND NATURALIZED GARDENS

Iris cristata

Dwarf Crested Iris · Crested Iris · Crested Dwarf Iris (USA)

This is a beautiful North American dwarf crested iris for a rock garden. During late spring, it bears 5-6·5cm (2-2½in) wide, lilac-purple flowers, whose white crests are tipped with orange.
Height: 15cm (6in)
Spread: 15-20cm (6-8in)
Cultivation: Slightly moist, fertile soil enriched with leafmould is needed, either slightly acid or neutral. A sheltered position in light shade is desirable.
Propagation: After flowering, lift and divide the plants, replanting the rhizomes immediately.

Below: **Iris cristata**
This dwarf crested iris from the Southern States of North America needs slightly acid or neutral soil in light shade. It is well suited to planting in a peat bed.

Iris gracilipes

This crested iris belongs to the group of irises which have orchid-like flowers with cock's-comb crests instead of beards. This species is hardy, with slender, dark green leaves, and 2·5-5cm (1-2in) wide, lavender-pink flowers, which appear during mid and late spring.
Height: 20-25cm (8-10in)
Spread: 20-25cm (8-10in)
Cultivation: Fertile, moisture-retentive lime-free soil is essential, in a

sheltered and slightly shaded position. To ensure that the soil is rich in humus, top-dress it with well-decomposed compost in spring. Plant the rhizomes in the soil during late spring, just below the surface.
Propagation: It is easily increased by lifting and dividing the rhizomes in late spring. Other crested irises are best lifted, divided and replanted immediately after the flowers have faded, but this beautiful species is the exception to the rule.

Below: **Iris gracilipes**
This small crested iris displays pretty flowers in spring. It is ideal for planting in moist, acid soil, in a sheltered, slightly shaded position.

Iris kaempferi

Japanese Iris (USA)

This beardless iris belongs to a group that delights in moist soil. It displays deeply ribbed, deciduous, deep green leaves, and 10-20cm (4-8in) wide flowers in early summer. Many varieties and strains of this iris have been developed, with colours including blue, reddish-purple, pink and white. Some are completely one colour, while others have a mixture and a few reveal a netting of white or coloured veins.
Height: 60-90cm (2-3ft)
Spread: 45-60cm (1½-2ft)
Cultivation: Moist soil at the edge of an informal pool is best, but the roots

---

Iris gracilis is a dwarf iris that is ideal for a sheltered pocket in a rock garden. Alternatively, plant it among small acid-loving shrubs that offer shade and protection for the delicate flowers.

Iris kaempferi forms a bold display at the side of a pool, ideal as a backcloth for the pool itself and for bringing height to the pool surrounds. The large, bright flowers are best grown on their own.

should not be set in the water. Rich soil and an annual mulch of well-rotted compost are aids to success. Plant the rhizomes just below the surface during the spring or autumn.

Propagation: It is easily increased by lifting and dividing the rhizomes immediately flowering is over. At this time the plants can be easily lifted, even from very boggy soil. They must be replanted immediately.

Below: **Iris kaempferi**
This handsome beardless iris for moist soil at the edges of a pond has been bred in Japan to produce a wide range of flower forms and colours during early summer.

Above: **Iris reticulata 'Jeanine'**
This is a reliable bulbous iris for a rock garden or front of a border, flowering in late winter and early spring. It is suitable for chalky soil.

Iris reticulata

This well-known, small, bulbous iris is ideal for a rock garden or the front of a border. It is now available in a range of colours, but the true species is blue and violet, with or without orange blazes on the falls (the lower, drooping petals). Flowers appear during late winter and early summer. Good forms to look for include 'Cantab' (light blue), 'Clairette' (sky-blue), 'Royal Blue' (deep blue) and 'Jeanine' (violet blue).

Cultivation: Light, well-drained chalky soil in full sun or light shade suits it. Plant fresh bulbs in autumn, covering them with a 5-7·5cm (2-3in) layer of soil. This attractive bulb can also be grown indoors, but the plants should not be taken inside until the flower buds show colour. They are better grown in a cold greenhouse or conservatory.

Propagation: It is easily increased by lifting and dividing large clumps in late summer or early autumn. Large bulbs can be replanted, while smaller ones should be planted in a nursery bed and grown on for a few years until large enough to set out in their final, flowering positions.

Iris reticulata blends with many early spring-flowering plants, such as the Snowdrop (Galanthus nivalis), the yellow-flowered shrub *Mahonia japonica* and the Corsican Hellebore (*Helleborus lividus corsicus*).

ROCK AND NATURALIZED GARDENS

Above: **Lithodora diffusa 'Grace Ward'**
This is a beautiful prostrate plant for a rock garden, cascading over rocks to form a large mat of colour. This form produces intense blue flowers from mid-summer to early autumn.

Right: **Muscari armeniacum**
This stunningly attractive blue bulbous plant for spring colour, ideal for naturalizing under deciduous shrubs or as a path edging, is a native of Turkey and the Caucasus.

Below: **Pontederia cordata**
This eye-catching North American water plant brings height and colour late in summer. Eventually it forms a large clump, with purple-blue flowers.

Lithodora diffusa

(Lithospermum diffusum)

This superb hardy, spreading, mat-forming perennial for a rock garden, is often better known by its previous botanical name, even though this has been superseded. The creeping stems are covered with small, oval, dark green leaves, and the five-lobed, 12mm (½in) wide, deep blue flowers appear from mid-summer to early autumn. Two varieties are widely available: 'Heavenly Blue' (deep blue) and 'Grace Ward' (a beautiful intense blue).
Height: 7·5-10cm (3-4in)
Spread: 45-60cm (1½-2ft)
Cultivation: Light, well-drained, slightly acid soil rich in leafmould or peat suits it best, and a position in full sun will ensure success.
Propagation: It is not easy to increase, the exact time for taking the cuttings being critical. Take 4-6·5cm(1½-2½in) long heel cuttings after the first week in mid-summer. Insert them in boxes of equal parts peat and sharp sand and place in a cold frame. Ensure that the compost does not become dry.

Lithodora diffusa can be used with other prostrate plants, such as *Helianthemum nummularium* 'Beech Park Scarlet' and the blue-purple *Campanula portenschlagiana*.

Muscari armeniacum

Grape Hyacinth (UK and USA)

In spring, this well-known hardy bulb has the heads of its stems tightly clustered with bell-like, azure-blue to deep purple-blue flowers, which have whitish rims to their mouths. The narrow dark green leaves tend to spread and separate as the flowers appear. Several forms are available, such as 'Cantab' (pale sky blue), 'Heavenly Blue' (bright blue) and 'Blue Spike' (double and mid-blue). It is ideal for planting in large drifts under shrubs or in fine grass. When planted in a rock garden, it needs careful watching as it can soon spread and dominate choice plants.

Height: 18-23cm (7-9in)

Spread: 10-13cm (4-5in)

Cultivation: Any well-drained garden soil in full sun suits it. During late summer or early autumn, plant new bulbs 7·5cm (3in) deep.

Propagation: It often spreads quite easily by self-sown seedlings. Alternatively, large clumps can be lifted and divided when the leaves are yellowing. Replant them immediately.

Pontederia cordata

Pickerel Weed (UK and USA)

This is a hardy and vigorous herbaceous perennial for the edge of a garden pool, in water up to 23cm (9in) deep. The glossy, deep green heart-shaped leaves are borne on stiff, long, upright stems, with 5-10cm (2-4in) long heads of purple-blue flowers during late summer and into early autumn.

Height: 45-75cm (1½-2½ft)

Spread: 30-45cm (1-1½ft)

Cultivation: Rich, fibrous loam and a sunny position are needed, with the rhizomes covered by several inches of water. Planting is best done during late spring or early summer.

Propagation: It is best increased by lifting and dividing the rhizomes in late spring. Take care that they do not dry out. Also, make sure that the roots are submerged deeply until the plants are established.

Muscari armeniacum is a superb companion for Primroses and polyanthus. *Anemone blanda* can be added to this trio, and they can all be set like a multi-coloured ruff around a spring-flowering tree.

Pontederia cordata is ideal for the side of a formal pool, where its foliage spills out over the edges, softening and blending the structured elements with the pool and creating a bright splash of colour.

Primula vialii

A distinctive outdoor primula, this species has a rosette of large pale green narrow lance-shaped leaves and 7·5-13cm (3-5in) long, poker-like, dense spikes of slightly scented, lavender-blue flowers during mid-summer.

Height: 20-30cm (8-12in)
Spread: 23-30cm (9-12in)
Cultivation: Moisture-retentive fertile soil and light shade suit it. The soil must not dry out during summer, but at the same time should never be waterlogged.
Propagation: Established plants can be divided and replanted directly after the flowers have faded. However, it is often better to sow seeds in summer in loam-based compost and place them in a cold frame. Shade the boxes and subsequent seedlings from strong sunlight. When they are large enough to handle, prick off the seedlings into boxes and replace them in the cold frame. Plant them out into the garden in spring.

Right: **Primula vialii**
This beautiful Chinese primula bears poker-like spikes of slightly-scented lavender-blue flowers in mid-summer. When planted in a large drift, perhaps at the side of an informal garden pool, it is a stunning sight in flower.

Primula denticulata

Drumstick Primula · Drumstick Primrose (UK)

This popular hardy primula produces a dramatic garden display. The pale-green lance-shaped leaves form a compact rosette at its base, while during spring and into early summer the stems bear 5-7·5cm (2-3in) wide globular flower heads in colours ranging from deep purple to deep lilac and carmine. A white form 'Alba' is also available, while 'Ruby' is rose-purple.

Height: 23-30cm (9-12in)
Spread: 20-25cm (8-10in)
Cultivation: Moisture-retentive loam,

Above: **Primula denticulata**
This is the well-known Drumstick Primula, with globular heads of flowers during spring and into early summer. It is an excellent and reliable plant for beginners to gardening and seldom fails to attract attention.

enriched with leafmould, and a lightly shaded site are ideal.
Propagation: Sow seeds in mid-summer in pots of loam-based compost and place them in a cold frame. When they are large enough to handle, prick out the seedlings into boxes of compost and plant them out into the garden in autumn.

Puschkinia scilloides

(Puschkinia libanotica · P. sicula · Adamsia scilloides)
Striped Squill (UK)

This exceptionally attractive small hardy bulb suits many sites in the garden, from naturalizing in low, fine grass to planting in rock gardens or alongside narrow borders at the bases of walls. The mid-green, strap-like leaves are surmounted by arching stems, bearing up to six, silvery-blue, bell-shaped, 12mm (½in) long flowers during spring.

Height: 13-20cm (5-8in)
Spread: 7·5-10cm (3-4in)
Cultivation: Any light garden soil and a position in sun or partial shade

Primula denticulata is an amenable plant that mingles happily with many other spring-flowering types, such as *Anemone blanda*, the Grape Hyacinth (*Muscari armeniacum*), Daffodils and Primroses.

Primula vialii needs careful positioning in a garden, as its distinctive flowers are best not forced to compete with other low-growing plants. It is best given a bed or corner to itself.

Ramonda myconi

(Ramonda pyrenaica)

A hardy, dainty-flowered, rosette-forming rock-garden plant with evergreen, deep green, crinkled and rusty-haired leaves. The 2·5-4cm (1-1½in) wide, lavender-blue flowers with golden stamens are borne in late spring, several to a stem.
Height: 10-15cm (4-6in)
Spread: 20-25cm (8-10in)
Cultivation: Well-drained leafmould-enriched garden soil and a cool position on the north side of a slope suit it best. Do not allow the soil to dry out. It is also good for planting in rock crevices or between peat blocks.
Propagation: During autumn or early spring, sow seeds in a tray of a loam-based compost and place it in a cold frame. When they are large enough to handle, prick out the seedlings into small pots and replace them in the frame. Plant them out into the garden when they are well established. Alternatively, take leaf-cuttings in mid-summer. They take about six weeks to produce roots. Pot up immediately.

assure success. Plant the bulbs in autumn, 5cm (2in) deep, and leave them where they are for many years.
Propagation: After flowering and when the foliage has died down, lift and divide congested clumps. Remove and dry the bulbs, replanting them in autumn.

Right: **Puschkinia scilloides**
This attractive bulbous plant produces silvery-blue flowers in spring on arching stems. It tolerates sun or partial shade, and, once planted, can be left undisturbed for many years.

Puschkinia scilloides displays such soft-coloured flowers that they can be blended with many other rock garden plants. The vivid mauve flowers of *Viola labradorica* are highlighted by puschkinia's flowers.

Ramonda myconi, with its wrinkled rusty-coloured leaves and blue flowers, is so distinctive that it is best given plenty of space to reveal itself. A background of washed shingle helps to show it off even better.

ROCK AND NATURALIZED GARDENS

Above: **Rhododendron 'Blue Tit'**
This dwarf dome-shaped evergreen shrub has funnel-shaped lavender-blue flowers that darken with age. It is ideal for a rock garden, creating height and dramatic colour in late spring and early summer.

Above: **Scilla sibirica 'Spring Beauty'**
These vivid-blue flowers appear in spring, delighting in moist but well-drained soil in a wild garden or boggy area around a pond. They can grow beneath shrubs.

Right: **Scilla tubergeniana**
Although its colouring is not so striking as Scilla sibirica, it does form a soil-covering mass of colour, and is ideal for planting in rock gardens or under deciduous shrubs, where it brings early colour.

Rhododendron 'Blue Tit'

A hardy and reliable small-leaved evergreen dwarf rhododendron for a rock garden, peat bank or heather garden. It forms a dense, rounded shrub with small funnel-shaped lavender-blue flowers at the tips of the branches during late spring and into early summer. As the flowers age, they become dark blue.
Height: 90cm (3ft)
Spread: 90cm-1·2m (3-4ft)
Cultivation: Moisture-retentive acid soil in light shade under trees is best. To keep the soil moist, mulch the surface with well-decomposed compost in spring.
Propagation: After flowering, take cuttings of young shoots with heels and insert them in pots of peaty compost. Place them in a cold frame and grow on until ready for planting out in the garden.

Scilla sibirica

Siberian Squill (UK and USA)

This popular, hardy, spring-flowering bulbous plant has wide, dark green, strap-shaped leaves, which appear in spring. These are followed by

several stems, each bearing two to five brilliant blue, nodding, bell-shaped flowers. The blue is so dominant that if often appears to overwhelm other plants. It is the form 'Spring Beauty' (often known as 'Atrocaerulea'), with deep blue flowers, that is most frequently seen.
Height: 13-15cm (5-6in)
Spread: 7·5-10cm (3-4in)
Cultivation: Well-drained but moist soil in full sun or slight shade suits it. Set the bulbs 5-7·5cm (2-3in) deep in late summer.
Propagation: Established clumps can be lifted and divided in autumn; otherwise they are best left alone.

Right: **Rhododendron 'Blue Star'**
This dominantly coloured dwarf rhododendron creates a bold display. Several other varieties are noted for their flowers, too, including 'Blue Diamond', with clusters of rich lavender-purple flowers in spring. It is slow-growing and only 1m (3½ft) high.

Many other **blue-flowered rhododendrons** can be used in small gardens, such as 'Blue Diamond' (lavender-blue), 'Blue Chip' (brilliant blue), 'Praecox' (rose-purple) and 'Saint Merryn' (intense blue).

Scilla sibirica is superb for planting under *Daphne mezereum* 'Alba' or among the lilac-flowered carpet provided by a mass planting of the diminutive Violet Cress (*Ionopsidum acaule*).

Above: **Sisyrinchium bermudianum**
This is a beautiful plant for a rock garden, where it readily increases itself by self-sown seedlings which grow in the gaps between paving stones, as well as other inhospitable places in the garden.

Scilla tubergeniana

This attractive hardy bulbous plant from North-west Iran displays its pale blue or white flowers in early spring. At first, the flowers are bell-like, but later they flatten amid wide strap-like glossy bright green leaves. In addition to this species and *Scilla sibirica*, the 23-30cm (9-12in) high Cuban Lily (*Scilla peruviana*) is well worth growing in the border. During early summer, this scilla bears crowded heads of attractive, star-shaped blue flowers.

Height: 7·5-10cm (3-4in)
Spread: 7·5-10cm (3-4in)
Cultivation: Moist but well-drained soil in full sun or light shade suits it best. Plant the bulbs 7·5cm (3in) deep in late summer.
Propagation: Congested clumps can be lifted and divided in autumn. Alternatively, it can be raised from seed, but this takes up to five years to produce flowering-sized plants.

Sisyrinchium bermudianum

Blue-eyed Grass (UK and USA)

A hardy member of the iris family, with stiff and erect narrow grey-green leaves and branched stems. At their tips, the stems bear 12mm (½in) wide, star-shaped, satin-blue, yellow-centred flowers from early summer until late autumn. It is best grown in a rock garden.

Height: 20-25cm (8-10in)
Spread: 15-23cm (6-9in)
Cultivation: Well-drained, humus-enriched garden soil and a sunny position ensure success. In autumn, cut off dead leaves and flowered stems.
Propagation: It tends to readily increase itself by seed, and these seeds can be gathered and potted up for planting out at a later stage when better developed. Bring them on in a cold frame and set them out in the garden when they are growing strongly.

Scilla tubergiana has subtly coloured flowers, and can be mixed with other small bulbs, like the Winter Aconite (*Eranthis hyemalis*) and Snowdrop (*Galanthus nivalis*), without being dominated by or overwhelming them.

Sisyrinchium brachypus is another delightful species, with 18mm (¾in) wide, star-shaped, yellow flowers, borne from early summer onwards on relatively low plants, only 15cm (6in) high.

ROCK AND NATURALIZED GARDENS

Tecophilaea cyanocrocus

Chilean Crocus (UK and USA)

This beautiful, crocus-like, South American bulbous plant is not fully hardy in temperate regions, but is well worth growing for its gorgeous 4cm (1½in) long flowers, with deep blue to purple petals and white throats, which appear in spring.
Height: 10-13cm (4-5in)
Spread: 13-15cm (5-6in)
Cultivation: In its native Chile, it grows on stony, well-drained slopes. In the garden, therefore, it needs well-drained sandy soil, and a warm and sunny position. It grows outdoors only in mild areas, free from severe frost. In wet climates it needs protection with cloches during winter. Plant the corms in mid-autumn.
Propagation: It is not easily increased and usually the plants produce few cormlets. When grown in a cool greenhouse, the plants can be removed from the pots in autumn and the cormlets potted up.

Above: **Tecophilaea cyanocrocus**
A low-growing rock garden plant that thrives in a well-drained, sheltered and warm position. Excessive moisture in winter will harm it. The richly-coloured, crocus-like flowers appear in spring.

Below: **Veronica teucrium 'Trehane'**
This beautiful rock garden plant has golden-yellow leaves, and bears spires of pale blue flowers during most of summer. Its foliage blends well with rocks, harmonizing with the colour of the stone.

Veronica teucrium

This hardy alpine veronica forms a clump of upright stems bearing mid to dark green, toothed lance-shaped leaves, with 5-7·5cm (2-3in) long spikes of sky blue flowers during most of summer. Several cultivated varieties are available, which are lower growing than the original species: these include 'Trehane' (golden-yellow leaves and pale blue flowers), 'Shirley Blue' (deep blue flowers) and 'Rosea' (rose-pink flowers and only 15cm (6in) high).
Height: 23-38cm (9-15in)
Spread: 45-60cm (1½-2ft)
Cultivation: Ordinary well-drained garden soil and a sunny position are essential for continued success.
Propagation: During spring, lift and divide large clumps. Alternatively, take cuttings from mid to late summer and insert them in pots of equal parts peat and sharp sand. When they are rooted, pot up the cuttings and overwinter them in a cold frame before planting them out in the garden.

Tecophilaea cyanocrocus is a warmth-loving bulb that does well in situations similar to those needed by the tender South African nerines and the beautiful Algerian Iris (*Iris unguicularis*), also known as *Iris stylosa*.

Veronica teucrium is ideal for planting at the front of borders as well as rock gardens, especially mixed with yellow and white flowers. In a rock garden it blends well with the lemon-yellow *Hypericum olympicum* 'Citrinum'.

Above: **Viola cornuta**
This beautiful hardy viola is ideal for well-drained but moist and fertile soils in sun or slight shade. It is perfect for bringing colour to path edges or in rock gardens. There is also a white-flowered form.

Viola cornuta

Horned Violet (UK and USA)

A reliable, lusty and robust violet from the Pyrenees, the Horned Violet bears lavender or violet-coloured flowers that provide early or mid-summer colour. The 2·5cm (1in) wide, spurred flowers are borne above the mid-green, oval leaves, which have rounded teeth. Several forms are available, including 'Minor' (lavender-blue), 'Jersey Gem' (blue-purple) and 'Alba' (white).
Height: 10-30cm (4-12in)
Spread: 30-38cm (12-15in)
Cultivation: Fertile, well-drained but moist soil in full sun or slight shade suits it best. Pick off dead flowers to encourage the development of further blooms.
Propagation: During spring or summer, sow seeds 6mm (¼in) deep in a prepared seedbed outdoors. When they are large enough to handle, thin the seedlings to 25-30cm (10-12in) apart. In autumn, transfer them to their flowering positions.

Further plants to consider

Meconopsis betonicifolia
(Meconopsis baileyi)
Himalayan Blue Poppy (UK) · Blue Poppy (USA)
Height: 90cm-1·5m (3-5ft)   Spread: 45cm (1½ft)
A distinctive hardy herbaceous perennial for a moist, shaded area, producing 6·5-7·5cm (2½-3in) wide, sky blue flowers during mid-summer.

Meconopsis grandis
Height: 45-60cm (1½-2ft)   Spread: 45cm (1½ft)
A hardy herbaceous perennial for a moist and lightly-shaded area, bearing 10-13cm (4-5in) wide, rich blue to purple flowers during early summer.

Meconopsis quintuplinervia
Harebell Poppy (UK and USA)
Height: 23-30cm (9-12in)   Spread: 30-38cm (12-15in)
A spreading dwarf perennial, with mid-green leaves and 5cm (2in) wide, nodding, lavender-blue or purple flowers during early summer.

Mertensia virginica
Virginian Cowslip (UK)
Bluebells · Virginia Bluebell · Virginia Cowslip · Roanoke-bells (USA)
Height: 30-60cm (1-2ft)   Spread: 45cm (1½ft)
A hardy herbaceous perennial with blue-grey, lance-shaped leaves and pendulous clusters of purple-blue flowers in early summer.

Omphalodes verna
Blue-eyed Mary (UK) · Creeping Forget-me-not (USA)
Height: 13-15cm (5-6in)   Spread: 30-38cm (12-15in)
A spreading herbaceous perennial for a rock garden or woodland. From early spring to early summer, it bears white-throated, bright blue flowers, 12mm (½in) wide.

Primula juliae
Height: 7·5-10cm (3-4in)   Spread: 25-30cm (10-102in)
A delightful mat-forming primula with yellow-eyed, 18mm (¾in) wide, reddish-purple flowers in spring and early summer.

Primula marginata
Height: 10-13cm (4-5in)   Spread: 20-25cm (8-10in)
A beautiful alpine primula with grey-green, silver-edged leaves and numerous heads of 18-25mm (¾-1in) wide, fragrant, lavender-blue flowers in spring. The form 'Linda Pope' has deep lavender-blue flowers.

Pulsatilla vulgaris
(Anemone pulsatilla)
Pasque Flower (UK and USA)
Height: 25-30cm (10-12in)   Spread: 30-38cm (12-15in)
A beautiful and highly memorable hardy herbaceous perennial with mid-green, fern-like leaves and 5-7·5cm (2-3in) wide, cup-shaped, purple flowers with bright centres during spring and early summer.

Viola cornuta is robust enough to be set at the front of a border with a backing of white flowers. Alternatively, position it in a rock garden, where it can trail over the rocks and merge with other plants.

CHAPTER THREE

CONTAINER GARDENING

Once the spring-flowering bulbs burst into bloom it is possible to believe that spring has really begun and that Nature is not going to play any perverse tricks. Although a slight frost is still possible in late spring, bulbs appear to withstand a few degrees of below-freezing temperatures without coming to any harm.

Bulbs for spring displays are often sold in ready-to-plant mixtures that include dominant blues as well as colour contrasts in yellow and white. Selections for window-boxes and troughs include blue Grape Hyacinths, yellow *Crocus chrysanthus*, red dwarf species tulips and pink hyacinths. For urns and tubs, where extra height is acceptable, you might choose blue hyacinths, yellow *Narcissus cyclamineus* 'February Gold', the Darwin Hybrid tulip 'Apeldoorn' (about 60cm (2ft) high with rich red flowers), blue Grape Hyacinths and blue crocuses.

In large tubs a relatively flat spring display looks best, so try polyanthus with the bright blue Grape Hyacinth. Set the polyanthus in a circle towards the outside of the tub, with the centre reserved for a random mixture of Grape Hyacinths and polyanthus. This combination looks stunning positioned against a white-coloured wall in full sun. For extra height plant blue Forget-me-nots interspersed with white narcissi. You could also buy a large herb or strawberry-growing pot, which has cup-like holes around the outside, and plant a living picture of crocuses at the sides with a hyacinth and several crocuses at the top.

In window-boxes and troughs a montage of small white species tulips, blue Grape Hyacinths and a small-leaved variegated ivy is appealing. Another attractive combination is blue stocks, white Marguerites and the silver-leaved *Senecio bicolor*.

Containers can look superb filled with single plants of one hue, rather than a mixture of colours and flowers. Examples include a white urn planted with Grape Hyacinths, agapanthus in a wooden barrel, and violas in large-topped weathered containers. When planting only one species it is essential to give thought to the style of the container, as both will be competing for attention and they must be in harmony.

Left: **Petunias** *are ideal in containers, smothering the surface with flower heads. Remove dead flower heads regularly to ensure a continuing display throughout summer.*

Cultivation: Well-drained, fertile soil and a sheltered sunny position suit it. Spring is the best time to set the plants out in the open soil. You should cover the crowns with 5cm (2in) of soil. In containers, use a free-draining, loam-based compost. After flowering, cut the stems down to soil-level and cover the base of the plant with straw, bracken or peaty compost. Plants in containers are best placed in a cold, frost-free greenhouse during winter, both to protect the crowns from frost and to prevent the compost from becoming too wet.

Propagation: The easiest method is to lift and divide congested clumps in mid to late spring. Take care not to damage the roots.

Convolvulus tricolor

(Convolvulus minor)

This beautiful hardy bushy annual from Southern Europe has dark green wide lance-shaped leaves and rich blue trumpet-shaped 4cm (1½in) wide flowers with yellow or white throats from mid to late summer. Several superb varieties are available, including 'Blue Flash' at 23cm (9in) high with brilliant blue flowers with star-like white and yellow centres, and 'Royal Ensign' with a trailing habit and deep blue flowers displaying yellow and white centres. The shorter varieties include 'Rainbow Flash' at 15cm (6in) high. This is a new dwarf hybrid in a wide range of colours including blue, purple, pink and rose.

Height: 30-38cm (12-15in)
Spread: 2-25cm (8-10in)
Cultivation: Ordinary well-drained fertile garden soil and a sunny position suits them. Select a sheltered position, and the taller-growing types may require support from twiggy sticks. These delightful plants are ideal for window-boxes and troughs, or at the fronts of borders. And of course they can also be grown in annual borders.

Propagation: When growing for window-boxes or the fronts of borders, sow seeds in early spring in pots of loam-based compost at

---

Above: **Agapanthus campanulatus**
This is a beautiful plant for the garden as well as in large containers, where it quickly forms a strongly-coloured focal point.

Agapanthus campanulatus

African Lily (UK)

This fleshy-rooted nearly hardy herbaceous plant from Natal has mid-green, sword-like leaves that arise from its base. During late summer, it reveals pale blue flowers in crowded, rounded heads, borne at the tops of long, stiff stems above the foliage. Several varieties extend the colour range from white to amethyst. 'Isis' has large heads of lavender-blue flowers. Although not fully hardy, it is ideal for a large tub on a warm and sheltered patio, preferably facing south or west.

Height: 60-75cm (2-2½ft)
Spread: 38-45cm (15-18in)

Agapanthus campanulatus needs a large container all to itself—do not try mixing it with bulbous plants. These are best planted in separate containers and stood around the agapanthus.

Convolvulus tricolor brings a distinctive brightness to borders, happily blending with many annuals such as French and African Marigolds (*Tagetes erecta* and *T. patula*).

15°C (59°F). When they are large enough to handle, prick out the seedlings into boxes of loam-based compost and harden them off in a cold frame. Plant them out when all risk of frost has passed. Alternatively, sow seeds in late spring where the plants are to flower, 12mm (½in) deep. When large enough to handle, thin the seedlings to 23cm (9in) apart. For larger plants, sow seeds under cloches during late summer.

Right: **Convolvulus tricolor 'Rainbow Flash'**
This dwarf hybrid produces bright new flowers each morning, and is ideal for window-boxes, tubs and troughs. Other varieties are a good choice for annual and mixed borders.

Felicia bergeriana

Kingfisher Daisy (UK and USA)

This stunningly attractive half-hardy annual has a mat-forming habit and grey, hairy, lance-shaped leaves. The 18mm (¾in) wide, steel-blue flowers with gold centres appear from mid to late summer. It is ideal for growing in containers, such as tubs, troughs and window-boxes, as well as for positioning as an edging to paths or in a rock garden.
Height: 15cm (6in)
Spread: 15-20cm (6-8in)
Cultivation: Well-drained garden soil and a sheltered position in full sun suits it. When grown in containers use a well-drained loam-based compost.
Propagation: From early to mid-spring sow seeds thinly in pots of loam-based seed compost at 15°C (59°F). Prick out the seedlings into boxes of loam-based compost and harden them off in a cold frame. Set the plants out in the garden or in containers during late spring, after all risk of frost has passed.

Right: **Felicia bergeriana**
This is an eye-catching half-hardy annual ideal for growing in containers, as a path edging or in a rock garden. It is a South African plant that requires a sheltered and warm position.

Felicia bergeriana is neat and dwarf, making it suitable for inclusion in a potpourri of bright annuals in containers. These plants look best when viewed from above, so do not plant them in high window-boxes.

CONTAINER GARDENING

Hyacinthus orientalis

*Common Hyacinth · Garden
Hyacinth (UK)
Hyacinth · Dutch Hyacinth ·
Common Hyacinth (USA)*

These beautifully-scented bulbs are
equally at home whether in spring-
bedding schemes or in raised beds,
tubs, troughs and window-boxes.
The true species is no longer
generally grown and therefore it is
the larger-flowered Dutch Hyacinths
that are commonly seen. These
have elegant, scented, 10-15cm
(4-6in) high spires of wax-like
flowers in a wide range of colours,
including blue.

Height: 15-23cm (6-9in)

Spread: 10-15cm (4-6in)

Cultivation: Light, well-drained but
moisture-retentive soil suits it, and
when grown in a garden the bulbs
can be set in position, 13-15cm
(5-6in) deep, in autumn. This is
usually done after summer-flowering
plants have been removed from the
border or container. The bulbs are
left in position until after they flower,
then lifted and re-planted in an
out-of-the-way position where they
can be left undisturbed to flower
during the following and successive
years. When grown in containers,
use a loam-based compost, setting
the bulbs 13-15cm (5-6in) deep and
the same distance apart. Plant the
bulbs during autumn. When grown
in small-area containers—window-
boxes and troughs—take care to
ensure that the compost does not
become totally saturated with water
and then freeze for long periods
during winter. Large tubs usually
need less care and attention. After
flowering, the bulbs can be lifted and
planted among shrubs.

Propagation: Although hyacinths
can be raised from seeds, they take
up to six years to produce flowering-
sized bulbs by this method and even
then large-flowered types do not
always come true. It is therefore
much easier to buy flowering-sized
bulbs each year. Make sure you
buy your bulbs from a reputable
supplier who can guarantee
their quality.

Above: **Hyacinthus orientalis**
*The fragrance and colours of these
flowers can be better appreciated
when they are grown in containers
or raised beds. Such beds are easily
maintained by gardeners who are in
wheelchairs or have infirmities that
prevent them from bending. But
take care not to make the beds too
wide or the wrong height.*

Left: **Hyacinthus orientalis
'Ostara'**
*This is a deep purple-blue hyacinth
that produces a dense sea of colour
in borders or containers. It also
gives off a wonderful scent.*

Hyacinthus orientalis can be mixed with many other
bulbs, such as Grape Hyacinths, species tulips and
yellow crocuses. Another combination is blue crocuses,
Grape Hyacinths, species tulips and *Narcissus
cyclamineus* 'February Gold'.

Lobelia erinus

Edging Lobelia (USA)

This well-known reliable border edging and container plant is a half-hardy perennial invariably grown as a half-hardy annual. It has light green leaves, with masses of 6mm (¼in) wide pale blue or white flowers from early summer to the frosts of autumn. There are both trailing and compact border edging varieties, in a range of colours. The border-edging compact types include 'Cambridge Blue' (pale blue), 'Crystal Palace' (dark blue) and 'Mrs Clibran' (brilliant blue). Trailing types include 'Blue Cascade' (Cambridge blue) and 'Sapphire' (brilliant blue). Some varieties, such as 'Colour Cascade Mixed', reveal flowers in shades of blue, mauve, red and rose.

Height: 10-23cm (4-9in)
Spread: 10-15cm (4-6in)
Cultivation: Fertile, moist garden soil in a sheltered and sunny position in light shade suits it. In containers use well-drained loam-based compost.
Propagation: During late winter and early spring, sow seeds thinly and shallowly in pots of loam-based compost at 15°C (59°F). As soon as the seedlings can be handled,

Above: **Lobelia erinus**
These are indispensable half-hardy annuals for both containers and the garden. When growing them in containers, take care that the compost does not dry out during summer, especially when in shallow urns that hold relatively small amounts of compost.

prick them out into boxes of loam-based compost and harden them off in a cold frame. Move the plants to the garden when all risk of frost is over. To create an instant display of colour, plant lobelias in pots in a greenhouse.

Lobelia erinus blends with a wealth of other plants. A happy combination for containers is the pink-flowered fibrous-rooted *Begonia semperflorens* 'Pink Avalanche' and *Lobelia erinus* 'Cambridge Blue'.

Lobelia erinus is a good bed-fellow for geraniums in both containers and borders. Try pink pelargoniums with dark blue lobelia, or light or dark blue lobelia with French Marigolds (*Tagetes patula*) that display strong, rich colours.

CONTAINER GARDENING

Above: Myosotis alpestris 'Ultramarine'
The deep blue flowers of this Forget-me-not form a dense, low carpet. it is ideal for bringing colour to a rock garden or for planting in combination with spring-flowering yellow or orange bulbs.

Myosotis alpestris

(Myosotis rupicola/Myosotis sylvatica alpestris)
Forget-me-not (UK)
Forget-me-not · Scorpion Grass (USA)

This well-known hardy perennial, best treated as a hardy biennial, is ideal for planting in a container, a rock garden or a bed with spring-flowering bulbs where it forms a dense blanket of fragrant azure-blue flowers from late spring to mid-summer. Several exciting forms are available, including 'Ultramarine' (deep blue) and 'Blue Ball' (rich indigo-blue).
Height: 10-20cm (4-8in)
Spread: 15-23cm (6-9in)
Cultivation: Moderately fertile well-drained but moisture-retentive soil in light shade is best.
Propagation: During mid-summer, sow seeds 6mm (¼in) deep in a well-prepared seedbed. When they are large enough to handle, plant out the seedlings 15cm (6in) apart in nursery rows. If originally sown thinly they can just be thinned to 15cm (6in) apart. Keep the rows weeded and in autumn plant out into their flowering positions.

Right: Myosotis alpestris
This half-hardy annual is just as good in containers as in a border, perhaps as an edging. Even on its own it creates a dense splash of colour early in the year.

Myosotis alpestris can form an ideal low edging to beds, with a centre planting of the higher-growing (30cm/1ft) *Myosotis sylvatica* 'Blue Bird' and yellow or light orange tulips.

Further plants to consider

Campanula isophylla
Italian Bellflower · Star of Italy (UK)
Italian Bellflower · Falling Stars · Star of Bethlehem (USA)
Height: 15cm (6in)   Spread: 45-60cm (1½-2ft)
A trailing dwarf perennial, often used indoors as a house plant but hardy outside in hanging baskets in milder, sunny gardens. The heart-shaped mid-green leaves are borne amid a mass of tangled trailing stems, with 2·5cm (1in) wide star-shaped blue flowers appearing in late summer and into autumn.

Crocus chrysanthus
Height: 7·5cm (3in)   Spread: 6·5cm (2½in)
This delightful spring-flowering bulb brings colour to containers as well as to rock gardens. The species type is golden-yellow, but there are several blue or mauve forms, such as 'Blue Pearl' (pale blue on the outside, white within), 'Lady Killer' (purple-blue, edged white) and 'Princess Beatrix' (clear blue with a yellow base).

Crocus vernus
(Crocus neapolitanus)
Dutch Crocus (USA)
Height: 10-13cm (4-5in)   Spread: 7·5cm (3in)
This spring-flowering bulb is the parent of the large Dutch crocuses widely seen in gardens and containers. Blue, mauve and purple forms include 'Queen of the Blues' (lavender-blue), 'Negro Boy' (deep reddish-purple) and 'Purpureus Grandiflorus' (purplish-blue).

Exacum affine
Persian Violet (UK) · German Violet/Persian Violet (USA)
Height: 23-30cm (9-12in)   Spread: 20-25cm (8-10in)
Although usually grown as a plant for the home, in milder areas it can be used in containers on warm patios and terraces. From mid to late summer it displays fragrant, saucer-shaped 12-18mm (½-¾in) wide purple flowers with yellow stamens.

Fuchsia magellanica 'Pumila'
Height: 15-20cm (6-8in)   Spread: 25-30cm (10-12in)
This dwarf but spreading form of the hardy fuchsia is dainty and small enough for tubs, where it reveals red and purple flowers from mid to late summer and often into autumn.

Petunia x hybrida
Common Garden Petunia (USA)
Height: 25-38cm (10-15in)   Spread: 30-38cm (12-15in)
A half-hardy perennial best grown as a half-hardy annual, and used in containers as well as for bedding schemes in the garden. The large trumpet-shaped flowers from mid to late summer and often into autumn are available in a wide colour range, including mauve and blue. Among these are 'Resisto Blue' (mid-blue), 'Polaris' (deep blue with a white star), 'Blue Frost' (deep violet-blue with a pure white edge) and 'Blue Bedder' (blue). There are also many varieties with mixed colours, including blue, violet and mauve.

Myosotis alpestris also looks splendid when planted in a spring-flowering bedding display with creamy-yellow tulips and an occasional edging tuft of the lemon-gold *Alyssum saxatile* 'Citrinum'.

CHAPTER FOUR

WALL AND TRELLIS FILLERS

If sparkling tinsel highlights Christmas trees, then the garden equivalent for a trellis or pergola must be clematis, an extensive and varied group of climbers with flowers in many colours, including blue, mauve and purple. It is usually the large-flowered forms that are grown and one of the best is *Clematis* x *jackmanii*, with violet-purple flowers from mid-summer to autumn. This is especially attractive when grown with *Rosa* 'Mermaid', which has a rambling growth habit and large, single, sulphur-yellow flowers with deep amber stamens. Alternatively, this clematis looks splendid trained on a south-facing wall with a deep pink hydrangea at its base to create extra colour and provide a cool area of soil beneath for the roots of the clematis.

Clematis macropetala is one of the best of all clematis, with pendulous, double, light and dark blue flowers. It looks superb on a trellis, or scrambling out of a large and ornate container where it can merge with soft yellow flowers at the sides. Avoid strongly-coloured yellow plants as neighbours, since they may take on a dominant role instead of a supporting one.

When grown on a trellis, *Clematis macropetala* harmonizes with Common White Jasmine, *Jasminum officinale*, which produces a tangled mass of heavily-scented primrose-shaped white flowers from mid to late summer and often into autumn.

Laythyrus odoratus, the annual Sweet Pea cherished by flower arrangers, is a delight from mid to late summer, with its fragrant, highly-coloured flowers. It can be grown against a wall or up a tripod of canes and poles in a mixed border, where it provides a colourful focal point at eye level over a long period of time. Varieties worth considering include 'Larkspur' (pale blue), 'Noel Sutton' (deep rich mid-blue), 'Blue Danube' (deep mid-blue), 'Evensong' (soft blue), 'Blue Mantle' (deep violet-blue), 'The Doctor' (mauve), 'Eclipse' (deep mauve), 'Milestone' (bright velvety purple) and 'Royalist' (a beautiful rich purple).

Heights and spreads given for the plants in this chapter should only be taken as guides. If more space is available in one direction, the plant will adapt its growth accordingly.

Left: *The evergreen* **Ceanothus impressus** *grows best against a warm wall, where it creates a dominant display of deep blue flowers in spring.*

WALL AND TRELLIS FILLERS

Above: **Abutilon vitifolium**
This nearly-hardy shrub is a delight when set against a warm wall, where it will produce pale to deep mauve flowers in early and mid-summer. It likes the shade and protection afforded by nearby plants.

Abutilon vitifolium

Flowering Maple · Parlor Maple · Indian Maple (USA)

This beautiful deciduous shrub needs the protection of a warm wall, and grows best in milder climates. It develops downy, grey, three or five-lobed, palm-like leaves, and 5cm (2in) wide, pale to deep mauve flowers that open flat during early and mid-summer. The form 'Veronica Tennant' produces large flowers.
Height: 2·4-5m (8-15ft)
Spread: 1·5-2·1m (5-7ft)
Cultivation: Well-drained ordinary garden soil suits it; choose a position in slight shade and against a warm south or west-facing wall. No regular pruning is needed.
Propagation: It is best raised from seeds sown in mid-spring in loam-based compost at 16°C (61°F). When they are large enough to handle, prick out the seedlings into pots of loam-based compost and place them in a cold frame. Once the young plants are established, plant them out into a nursery bed for a couple of years.

Ceanothus impressus

Californian Lilac (UK)
Santa Barbara Ceanothus (USA)

This impressive evergreen shrub with a bushy habit is best grown against a warm wall. In the open it is not fully hardy. During spring, it reveals clusters of deep blue flowers amid small deep green leaves with deeply impressed veins.
Height: 2·4-3m (8-10ft)
Spread: 1·8-2·4m (6-8ft)
Cultivation: Light, fertile soil and a south or west-facing wall suit it best. It tolerates lime in the soil. No regular pruning is needed, other than initially shaping it when young.
Propagation: During late summer take half-ripe cuttings 6·5-7·5cm (2½-3in) long, inserting them in pots of equal parts peat and sharp sand. Place them in a propagation frame at 16°C (61°F). When the cuttings are rooted, pot them up into small pots of loam-based compost, setting them out in the garden when they are well grown.

Above: **Ceanothus impressus**
This beautiful evergreen Californian Lilac with small deep blue flowers in spring is not fully hardy and requires the protection of a south or west-facing wall. Ceanothus plants are native to North America, and come mostly from California.

Ceanothus rigidus

Californian Lilac (UK)
Monterey Ceanothus (USA)

This beautiful half-hardy evergreen wall shrub has distinctive wedge-shaped dark green leaves and 18-25mm (¾-1in) long clusters of purple-blue flowers during spring. It has a stiff, upright, compact growth habit, ideal for narrow or restricted areas.
Height: 1·8-3m (6-10ft)
Spread: 1·2-1·5m (4-5ft)
Cultivation: Light, fertile soil and a warm wall facing south or west ensure success. No regular pruning is needed, other than shaping during formative years.

Abutilon vitifolium is superb with yellow-flowered shrubs and trees, such as the glorious bright yellow daisy-like flowers of *Senecio* 'Sunshine' and the sweetly-scented yellow broom *Genista cinerea*.

Ceanothus impressus is superb when positioned under a high window or at the side of a lower one. Because of its neat, tight growth small late-winter and spring-flowering bulbs can be set at its base.

Propagation: During late summer, take half-ripe cuttings 6·5-7·5cm (2½-3in) long, inserting them in pots of equal parts peat and sharp sand. Place them in a propagation frame at 16°C (61°F). When the cuttings are rotted, pot them up into small pots of loam-based compost, planting them out in the garden when they are well grown.

Left: **Ceanothus rigidus**
This half-hardy evergreen shrub is ideal for a narrow, restricted area against a wall. It is a native of North America, and was first introduced into England in 1847.

Ceanothus thrysiflorus repens

Californian Lilac (UK)
Creeping Blueblossom (USA)

This hardy, vigorous, mound-forming evergreen shrub is ideal for planting against a wall, where it creates a dense screen of small shiny green leaves and light blue flowers in 7·5cm (3in) long clusters during early summer. This versatile shrub is also suitable for a large rock garden.
Height: 1·2-1·5m (4-5ft)
Spread: 1·5-1·8m (5-6ft)
Cultivation: Light, fertile soil and a south or west-facing position are best. No regular pruning is needed, other than an initial pruning during its formative years.
Propagation: During late summer, take half-ripe cuttings 6·5-7·5cm (2½-3in) long, inserting them in pots of equal parts peat and sharp sand. Place them in a propagation frame at 16°C (61°F). When they are rooted, pot up the cuttings into small pots of loam-based compost, and plant them in the garden when they are well grown. Ensure the young plants are well established.

Left: **Ceanothus thrysiflorus repens**
This hardy evergreen shrub is ideal for covering walls, especially under windows. It is lower growing than Ceanothus thrysiflorus, *which often reaches 3m (10ft) or more.*

Ceanothus rigidus is an excellent partner for low growing yellow-flowered shrubs that will continue the display into summer. Potentillas with their long flowering period are ideal for this purpose.

Ceanothus thrysiflorus repens creates a display of flowers at an earlier stage in its life than most ceanothus species—often when only two years old—so it is useful in new gardens or re-planned ones.

WALL AND TRELLIS FILLERS

Clematis—Large-flowered Types

These are some of the most spectacular and well-known of all climbers, producing a stunning display of large flowers during summer. They are derived from several forms, such as *florida, Jackmanii, lanuginosa, patens, texensis* and *viticella*. They are superb for training over pergolas, trellises or along wires tensioned against a wall. Most are single forms, but a few have double flowers. They include a wide range of colours, among which blue, mauve and purple can be found in the following types: 'Alice Fisk' (mauve), 'Barbara Dibley' (pansy-violet, with a carmine stripe), 'Belle of Woking' (pale mauve, and double), 'Gipsy Queen' (rich velvety violet-purple), 'Jackmanii Superba' (rich violet-purple), 'Marcel Moser' (mauve, with a deep carmine bar), 'Mrs Cholmondely' (pale blue), 'Percy Picton' (intense mauve, with a pink eye), 'President' — also called 'The President' — (deep purple-blue), 'Vyvyan Pennell' (deep violet-blue) and 'William Kennet' (lavender-blue).
Height: 1·2-3m (4-10ft)
Spread: 75cm-1·8m (2½-6ft)
Cultivation: Slightly alkaline, fertile, well-drained soil and an open and sunny position suit it, but the roots must be shaded from strong sunlight and you must not allow the soil to become dry during summer. Low-growing plants, as well as shrubs, can be positioned to keep the roots shaded and cool.
Propagation: They root readily from 10-13cm (4-5in) long stem cuttings taken in mid-summer and inserted in pots of equal parts peat and sharp sand, kept at 16°C (61°F). When the cuttings are rooted, pot them up singly into 7·5cm (3in) pots of loam-based compost and place them in a cold frame during winter. Transfer the cuttings to larger pots in spring or summer and plant them out into the garden in autumn. Alternatively, new plants can be obtained by layering low shoots in spring; they will root within a year or so.

Above: **Clematis 'Alice Fisk'**
This eye-catching clematis, which produces an abundance of large blooms, is a delight in a flower border when given a rustic pole for support. It does well in combination with other plants, which give its roots welcome shade.

Left: **Clematis 'Percy Picton'**
This is a relatively weak-growing type, but is ideal when planted in a small area. It is especially attractive when planted against a well-weathered wall.

Right: **Cobaea scandens**
This vigorous climber is grown as a half-hardy annual, and needs a sheltered and sunny position. The large bell-shaped purple flowers have distinctive green calyces (their outer, protective parts).

Clematis are easily trained up supports, as they hang by their leaves. Each leaf is formed of several leaflets held on long stalks, and it is these that secure the shoots in position.

Clematis are exciting when planted in association with roses, perhaps either side of an entrance. Blue clematis are eye-catching with yellow, creamy-white or pink roses, and low growing plants at the base to keep their roots cool.

Cobea scandens

Cathedral Bells · Cup and Saucer Vine (UK)
Mexican Ivy · Monastery Bells · Cup and Saucer Vine (USA)

This spectacular Mexican half-hardy perennial climber is best grown as a half-hardy annual. Fast-growing, it is ideal for trelliswork and pergolas, displaying mid to dark green leaves formed of three pairs of leaflets, and 6·5-7·5cm (2½-3in) long, bell-shaped, purple flowers with green, saucer-like calyces (outer, protective parts) from early to late summer. In a greenhouse it soon reaches 6m (20ft), but it does not grow so tall outdoors.

Height: 3-4·5m (10-15ft)
Spread: 1.8m (6ft)
Cultivation: Ordinary well-drained garden soil and a sunny, sheltered position are needed. If the soil is too rich, excessive growth is produced at the expense of flowers. Nip out the tips of young plants to encourage the development of sideshoots. Wire supports or wooden trelliswork are needed for support.
Propagation: During late winter and early spring, sow seeds singly 12mm (½in) deep in 7·5cm (3in) pots containing loam-based compost and kept at 16°C (61°F). When young plants are established move them to a cold frame to harden off. Plant them out into the garden after all risk of frost has passed.

Further plants to consider

Clematis alpina
(Atragene alpina)
Height: 1·5-1·8m) (5-6ft)   Spread: 90cm-1·2m (3-4ft)
An attractive, but weak-growing deciduous climber, with 2·5-3cm (1-1½in) wide, cup-shaped, violet-blue, late spring and early summer flowers that hang with their faces downwards. The form 'Frances Rivis' is free-flowering, with larger flowers.

Clematis macropetala
Height: 2·4-3·6m (8-12ft)   Spread: 1·2-1·5m (4-5ft)
A hardy, bushy, deciduous climber, related and quite similar to *C. alpina*. It produces 5-7·5cm (2-3in) wide, pendulous, light and dark blue flowers in early to mid-summer. The form 'Maidwell Hall' has deep blue flowers.

Clematis viticella
Height: 2·4-3·5m (8-12ft)   Spread: 1·5-1·8m (5-6ft)
A slender though bushy deciduous climber, with bell-shaped 5-6·5cm (2-2½in) wide blue, violet or reddish-purple flowers during mid to late summer and into early autumn. The form 'Abundance' has soft purple flowers and 'Royal Velours' has deep velvety-purple ones.

Passiflora caerulea
Common Passion Flower · Blue Passion Flower (UK) · Blue Passion Flower (USA)
Height: 6-7·5m (20-25ft)   Spread: 4·5-6m (15-20ft)
A vigorous evergreen climber, not fully hardy in cold, exposed areas. During summer, it has 7·5cm (3in) wide white-petalled flowers with blue-purple centres.

Solanum crispum
Chilean Potato Tree (UK)
Height: 4·5-6m (15-20ft)   Spread: 3·5-4·5m (12-15ft)
A hardy semi-evergreen bushy and scrambling climber, producing star-shaped purple-blue flowers with yellow anthers from mid-summer into autumn. The form 'Glasnevin' (syn. 'Autumnale') is hardier than the original type species.

Solanum jasminoides
Jasmine Nightshade (UK) · Potato Vine (USA)
Height: 3-4·5m (10-15ft)   Spread: 1·8-2·4m (6-8ft)
A rapid-growing, twining, evergreen climber, which has star-shaped pale blue flowers, with golden anthers in their centres, from mid-summer to autumn.

Wisteria floribunda 'Macrobotrys'
Japanese Wisteria (UK and USA)
Height: 7·5-9m (25-30ft)   Spread: 6-7·5m (20-25ft)
A spectacular hardy deciduous climber, displaying fragrant lilac-blue and purple flowers in drooping clusters up to 90cm (3ft) long in early to mid-summer. Arguably, it is the last word in climbers, and is certain to catch the eye.

Annual climbers have the advantage of quickly clothing trelliswork or pergolas and of producing variety each year—important in small gardens where change is needed to create continuing interest.

CHAPTER FIVE

TREES AND SHRUBS

Few shrubs or trees have received such acclaim as Lilac. *Syringa vulgaris*, an East European native, commonly known as Lilac and formerly as the Pipe Tree, has received the attentions of botanists and nurserymen for hundreds of years. A native of North Persia, it was introduced into Great Britain and North America via Vienna, around 1600. There are superb varieties to choose from, including double and single forms, some with French names, and some such as 'Maud Notcutt' suggesting the plant breeding endeavours of an important English nursery, Notcutt and Sons. Among these varieties are many blue and mauve forms, including 'Blue Hyacinth' (fragrant, mauve and opening to lavender-blue), 'Massena' (fragrant, with deep purple flowers), 'Firmament' (fragrant, single and lilac-blue) and 'Katherine Havemeyer' (fragrant, double lavender-blue, fading to soft lilac-pink).

Other shrubs that are strong contenders for summer and autumn colour include *Hebe* 'Midsummer Beauty', with long tassle-like heads of lavender-purple flowers throughout summer, and *Hebe* 'Autumn Glory', a low growing shrub with violet-blue flowers from mid-summer to autumn.

Blue-flowered shrubs are particularly in evidence in autumn, and include *Caryopteris* x *clandonense*, hydrangeas, hibiscus, *Ceratostigma willmottianum* and vincas. For autumn berries, try *Callicarpa bodinieri giraldii* (violet-blue berries), *Clerodendron trichotomum* (beautiful China blue berries with crimson calyces) and *Viburnum davidii* (bright turquoise berries on female plants).

Blue-foliaged conifers are useful for introducing year-through colour, and in addition to those described in this chapter there are *Chamaecyparis lawsoniana* 'Pembury Blue' (silvery-blue), *Juniperus horizontalis* 'Blue Chip' (bright blue) and *Juniperus squamata* 'Blue Star' (silvery-blue).

The heights and spreads given for plants in this chapter are those to be expected after twenty years in good soil.

Left: *The rich purple-leaved* **Berberis x ottawensis 'Purpurea'** *creates a contrast to the late spring white-flowered* Spiraea x cinerea *'Grefsheim' in this attractive shrub border.*

Ceanothus 'Gloire de Versailles'

(Ceanothus x delinianus 'Gloire de Versailles')

This hardy deciduous rather open shrub is one of the best known ceanothus plants for a border. The soft, fragrant, powder-blue flowers are borne in heads up to 20cm (8in) long from mid-summer until early autumn. It is best planted in a mixed border, where its long stems can splay out over lower-growing plants.
Height: 1·8-2·4m (6-8ft)
Spread: 1·5-2·1m (5-7ft)
Cultivation: Well-drained fertile soil in good light suits it. Because the flowers are borne on the new wood, the bush must be pruned hard in spring. Cut back the previous season's shoots almost to their points of origin. Follow this with an application of fertilizer to encourage the rapid growth of new shoots.
Propagation: During summer, take 7·5-10cm (3-4in) long half-ripe cuttings of the current season's growth, inserting them in pots of equal parts peat and sharp sand. Place them in a propagation frame at a temperature of 16°C (61°F). When they are rooted, pot up the cuttings into 7·5cm (3in) pots of loam-based compost and overwinter them in a cold frame. Plant them out in the garden in spring.

Cercis siliquastrum

Judas Tree (UK)
Judas Tree · Love Tree (USA)

A hardy, rounded, wide-spreading, deciduous tree from the Orient and Southern Europe, the Judas Tree is said to be the tree from which Judas Iscariot hanged himself after the betrayal of Jesus Christ. Whether or not this is true, there is no doubt that the tree is eye-catching and distinctive. It bears clusters of rich rose-purple flowers on bare branches in early summer. After the flowers have faded it develops rounded, glaucous-green leaves with heart-shaped bases. Subsequently, it produces attractive flat, green, pea-like pods tinted red when fully ripe.

Abies concolor 'Glauca Compacta'

This beautiful dwarf and compact conifer (often sold as *Abis concolor* 'Compacta') has an irregular shape and greyish-blue foliage. It is so slow-growing that even after twenty-five years it often reaches no more than 75cm (2½ft) high, with a 1m (3½ft) spread. It is ideal for a rock garden, or even in a large container.
Cultivation: Deep, well-drained, slightly acid soil suits it best. It prefers

Above: **Abies concolor 'Glauca Compacta'**
This is one of the best slow-growing dwarf conifers for a rock garden or container. Its greyish-blue foliage is very attractive and looks at its best when the tree is planted on its own or in a colour-contrasting group.

a warm, dry position. It is essential to avoid chalky soils.
Propagation: It is raised by grafting, a technique best left to nursery experts.

Abies concolor 'Violacea Prostrata' is another blue conifer ideal for a small garden. It is semi or totally prostrate, with strongly-coloured silver-blue foliage. Another prostrate blue form is *Abies procera* 'Glauca Prostrata'.

Ceanothus 'Gloire de Versailles' originated in France. In 1830 a breeding programme was initiated to raise new hybrids, and this shrub was one of the results. Most ceanothus shrubs with French-sounding names originated at that time.

Above: **Ceanothus 'Gloire de Versailles'**
This strikingly impressive deciduous shrub produces large heads of powdery-blue flowers on open stems from mid to late summer. It is best grown in a mixed border.

Height: 4·5-6m (15-20ft)
Spread: 3·5-4·5m (10-15ft)
Cultivation: Any good garden soil and a sunny position away from late spring frosts suit it. No regular pruning is needed.
Propagation: During spring, sow seeds in pots of loam-based compost kept at 13°C (55°F). When they are large enough to handle, pot up the seedlings singly in loam-based compost and plunge the pots up to their rims in a sheltered corner. Once established, the plants can be set out into the garden.

Right: **Cercis siliquastrum**
This is the well-known Judas Tree, which produces a wealth of colour along its bare branches in early summer. In colder areas it may require the protection of a south or west-facing wall.

Cercis siliquastrum is ideal for blending with late spring and early summer bulbs. Often, the tree becomes bare of low branches, and bright bulbs can create vital colour and interest around large and mature trees.

Corylus maxima 'Purpurea' produces its main burst of
foliage colour at eye height, and is useful for bringing
focal points to a shrub or mixed border. Its high stance
allows it to be underplanted with spring-flowering
bulbs—but not too close to its base.

Right: **Cotinus coggygria**
'Notcutt's Variety'
This superb hardy shrub with an
imposing stature bears beautiful
deep purple leaves. It produces its
best colour when planted in poor soil.

Corylus maxima 'Purpurea'

Purple-leaved Filbert (UK)

This is a rich-purple-leaved form of the Filbert, a native of Western Asia and Southern Europe. It is a deciduous shrub which has large, heart-shaped leaves. The whole shrub has an open, spreading growth habit, often becoming bare at its base. The parent form, *Corylus maxima*, was introduced into the British Isles in 1759 and soon became very popular for providing nuts. It also soon spread to North America and in 1833 several distinct varieties were known to be in cultivation. At one time it was widely grown in Europe, especially Italy and Spain, Early in the 1800s a plantation near Recus, Spain, yielded nuts that were shipped via Barcelona. They became known as Barcelona nuts.

Height: 2·4-3·5m (8-12ft)
Spread: 2·8-3m (8-10ft)
Cultivation: Any good well-drained garden soil and a sunny position, preferably sheltered from cold north and east winds, is suitable. During its early years, cut it back in late winter and early spring to encourage the development of shoots from around its base. Prune back by half the growth made the previous year. As the shrub develops, do not cut it back so severely. Throughout this period, cut out congested shoots from the centre of the shrub.
Propagation: Purple-leaved forms seldom come true from seeds and are therefore best increased by layering low growing shoots in autumn.

Left: **Corylus maxima 'Purpurea'**
This is a useful shrub for bringing colour-contrasting foliage to a garden throughout summer. It is a reliable plant, but is best given shelter from cold east and north winds.

Cotinus coggygria 'Notcutt's Variety'

This hardy deciduous shrub has eye-catching deep purple leaves that never lose their freshness and are ultimately semi-translucent. It also bears feathery purple flowers during mid-summer.
Height: 3·5-4·5m (12-15ft)
Spread: 3-3·5m (10-12ft)
Cultivation: Any good well-drained garden soil and a position in full sun suit it. Avoid rich soils, as it produces the best colour when in poor conditions. No regular pruning is needed, other than initially shaping the plant when young.
Propagation: During late summer, take 10-13cm (4-5in) long heel cuttings, inserting them in pots of equal parts peat and sharp sand. Place the pots in a cold frame and during spring set out the young plants into a nursery bed until they are large enough to be planted out in the garden. Keep the nursery bed free from weeds.

Cotinus coggygria 'Notcutt's Variety' will produce a
large specimen shrub on a lawn or as a backcloth for
colour-contrasting plants. For small gardens, *C. c.*
'Royal Purple' is better, growing to 3m (10ft) in height
and the same width.

TREES AND SHRUBS

Hydrangea macrophylla

Common Hydrangea (UK)
French Hydrangea · Hortensia (USA)

This well-known deciduous and rounded shrub from Japan and China has oval, slightly pointed, coarsely-toothed light green leaves. The flower-heads appear from mid to late summer. There are two forms: *Hortensia* types and the

Lacecaps. The *Hortensia* forms have large globose heads, while the *Lacecaps* display flat flower heads formed almost entirely of sterile flowers with a flat disc-like corymb. In the centre there is an area of tiny fertile flowers, and this has a marginal ring of ray florets which are sterile. The form 'Blue Wave' is a good example of this type.
Height: 1·5-1·8m (5-6ft)
Spread: 1·5-1·8m (5-6ft)

Cultivation: Slightly acid, light, well-drained but moisture-retentive soil is best. Acid soil is essential to ensure that blue varieties remain blue. Pink varieties also produce blue colours when given an acid soil and an aluminium sulphate dressing.
Propagation: From late spring to mid-summer, take cuttings 7·5cm (3in) long. Remove the lower leaves and cut the bases just below leaf joints. Insert them in pots of equal

Hydrangea macrophylla is ideal for forming a backcloth to a large lawn, where it provides colour over a long period. In such a position, a *Hortensia* type is best. The *Lacecaps* perform better in a naturalized garden setting.

88

parts peat and sharp sand and place them in a cold frame. When the cuttings are rooted, pot them up into an acid compost and plunge the pots to their rims in a nursery bed until they are ready to plant out into the garden.

Left: Hydrangea macrophylla
Hortensia hydrangeas are reliable garden favourites, creating a dominant display of mop-like heads from mid to late summer.

Right: Hydrangea macrophylla 'Blue Wave'
This vigorous Lacecap hydrangea provides flowers in shades of blue and pink throughout the summer months. It grows well in slight shade.

Lavandula stoechas

French Lavender (UK)
French Lavender · Spanish Lavender (USA)

This hardy evergreen shrub is native to the Mediterranean region. It has narrow, grey-green leaves and distinctive, deep purple, tubular flowers borne on 2·5-5cm (1-2in) long four-angled spikes during early to mid-summer. It is characterized by tufted purple bracts (modified leaves) borne at the tops of the flower spikes.

Height: 30-45cm (1-1½ft)
Spread: 45-60cm (1½-2ft)
Cultivation: Light, well-drained soils and an open and sunny position suit it. It is not as hardy as the English Lavender and during severe winters can be seriously damaged in exposed areas.
Propagation: During late summer, take 7·5cm (3in) long cuttings and insert them in pots of equal parts peat and sharp sand. Place them in a cold frame. Pot them up when they are rooted and plant them out into the garden in spring.

Right: Lavandula stoechas
This pretty lavender has distinctive deep purple flowers topped by purple bracts (modified leaves) that persist long after the actual flowers have faded.

Lavandula stoechas brings height and colour to a rock garden. Even after the flowers have faded, the grey-green leaves provide an attractive feature. Cover the soil with stone chippings to add extra interest and stop soil splashing on the leaves.

TREES AND SHRUBS

Above: **Picea pungens 'Pendula'**
With careful training and pruning, this often unpredictable conifer can be persuaded to develop a superb weeping shape and to create an exciting focal point in any garden.

Left: **Picea pungens 'Koster'**
This is one of the best blue spruces, with a neat pyramidal habit. It looks especially attractive in spring when the young and fresh growths appear on the branches.

Picea pungens 'Koster'

Koster's Blue Spruce (UK)

This distinctive form of the Colorado Spruce has intensely blue foliage and a neat growth habit, forming an upright and pyramidal shape up to 2·1m (7ft) high and 1m (3½ft) wide after ten years. During spring, it is further enhanced by pale blue tufts of new growth.

Height: 9m (30ft)
Spread: 3m (10ft)
Cultivation: Deep, moist soil—acid or neutral—is needed. A position in full sun or slight shade suits it best.
Propagation: It is grafted onto stocks of *Picea pungens* to produce a distinctive upright form. The cost to nurserymen of this time-consuming technique accounts for the high price they will ask for young plants of this lovely variety.

Picea pungens 'Pendula'

This distinctive blue conifer—often known as *Picea pungens* 'Glauca Pendula'—sometimes has an erratic shape but can be recognized by its down-swept branches and glaucous-blue leaves. During spring, the young growths are tufted and pale blue. It often produces two leading shoots: one needs to be trained upright, while the other trails downwards.

Height: 3-5·4m (10-18ft)
Spread: 3-5·4m (10-18ft)
Cultivation: Moist, deep soil—acid or neutral—is best, and a position in slight shade or full sun.
Propagation: It needs to be grafted onto a stock of *Picea pungens*, so the plants are often expensive to buy, as with *P. pungens* 'Koster'.

Picea pungens 'Thomsen'

This eye-catching blue spruce has an upright, cone-like growth habit and branches packed with silvery-blue foliage. During spring, it develops a fresh growth of very pale silver-blue that contrasts with the older and darker foliage. It forms a small to medium-sized tree, reaching only 2·1m (7ft) high and 1m (3½ft) wide after ten years.

Height: 9m (30ft)
Spread: 3m (10ft)
Cultivation: Moist deep soil—acid or neutral—is best, and a position in slight shade or full sun.
Propagation: It is a grafted form and therefore plants tend to be expensive. Raising new plants is best left to nurserymen.

Right: **Picea pungens 'Thomsen'**
This is a beautiful blue spruce with a cone-shaped outline. The foliage is thick and the needles long. It grows steadily into a strong, upright shape.

Picea pungens 'Koster' brings height to a small planting of heathers or the edge of a small rock garden. Eventually it forms a large plant, but up to the age of 15-20 years, it is quite suitable for a small area.

Picea pungens 'Pendula' must be given space and an open situation where other plants do not compete for attention. For colour contrast, set it in a sea of Heather (*Calluna vulgaris*), selecting forms with gold-tinted foliage.

Further plants to consider

Hebe 'Autumn Glory'
Height: 60-90cm (2-3ft)   Spread: 75cm-1m (2½-3½ft)
A well-known evergreen hybrid shrub, with purple stems displaying dark green leaves. From mid-summer to autumn, it bears violet-purple flowers in spikes 4cm (1½in) long.

Hebe x andersonnii 'Variegata'
Height: 90cm (3ft)   Spread: 60-90cm (2-3ft)
A beautiful double-value somewhat tender evergreen shrub with mid-green and cream leaves. The soft mauve flowers borne in dense spikes 7·5-13cm (3-5in) long appear from mid-summer to autumn. It is ideal for setting in a mixed border, where it creates attention throughout the year.

Hibiscus syriacus 'Blue Bird'
Shrubby Mallow (UK) · Althaea · Rose of Sharon (USA)
Height: 1·8-2·4m (6-8ft)   Spread: 1·2-1·8m (4-6ft)
A hardy deciduous shrub, with rich green leaves and mid-blue, 7·5cm (3in) wide flowers from mid to late summer and often into autumn. The form 'Coeleste' has deep blue flowers, and 'Mauve Queen' has mauve flowers that reveal maroon centres.

Paulownia tomentosa
Princess Tree · Karri Tree (USA)
Height: 6-7·5m (20-25ft)   Spread: 3·5-4·5m (12-15ft)
A hardy deciduous tree, with mid-green heart-shaped leaves and lavender-blue flowers in early summer.

Teucrium fruticans
Shrubby Germander (UK)
Height: 1·2-1·5m (4-5ft)   Spread: 90cm-1·2m (3-4ft)
A somewhat tender evergreen shrub, only really suitable for warm areas. The greyish-green leaves are fragrant, with two-lipped, lavender-blue flowers appearing from mid to late summer.

Vinca major
Greater Periwinkle (UK)
Greater Periwinkle · Blue Buttons · Band Plant (USA)
Height: 15-30cm (6-12in)   Spread: 90cm-1·2m (3-4ft)
A well-known trailing and mat-forming evergreen sub-shrub, with glossy mid-green leaves. During spring and early summer, and often repeatedly into autumn, it produces 2·5-3cm (1-1¼in) wide, purple-blue flowers.

Vinca minor
Lesser Periwinkle (UK)
Lesser Periwinkle · Common Periwinkle · Myrtle · Running Myrtle (USA)
Height: 5-10cm (2-4in)   Spread: 90cm-1·2m (3-4ft)
A spreading, mat-forming evergreen sub-shrub, with 18-25mm (¾-1in) wide, blue flowers during spring and mid-summer, and often into autumn.

Picea pungens 'Thomsen' is superb when positioned several metres in front of yellow-foliaged conifers or in an open situation with clear sky behind. Take care not to cramp it with other conifers set too close, as this will spoil its shape.

INDEX

COMMON NAMES
Names in *italic* type are those used in North America

INDEX

LATIN NAMES

CREDITS

Photographers
The majority of the photographs in this book have been taken by Eric Crichton © Salamander Books Ltd.

Copyright in the following photographs belongs to the suppliers:
Pat Brindley: 51
Eric Crichton: 18, 21 (Top right), 35, 38/39, 41 (Top left), 55 (Bottom), 59 (Top), 60/61 (Top), 71 (Bottom), 72 (Bottom), 74, 78 (Top right), 85 (Top left), 89 (Top)
Peter McHoy: 27, 43
Harry Smith Photographic Collection: 32 (Top left), 59 (Bottom)
David Squire: Front Cover, 6, 7, 10/11, 11, 12, 13, 14/15, 16 (Top right), 22 (Top right), 23 (Bottom), 33 (Top), 44/45, 46/47, 48 (Bottom), 49 (Bottom), 60/61 (Bottom), 64/65, 68/69, 72 (Top), 73 74/75, 76/77, 78 (Top left), 79 (Top), 79 (Bottom), 80 (Top), 80 (Bottom), 82/83, 86, 88, Back Cover
Michael Warren: 87

Artists
Copyright of the artwork illustrations on the pages following the artists' names is the property of Salamander Books Ltd.
Nicki Kemball: 6/7, 12/13
Steve Linds (Linden Artists): 8, 8/9, 9, 10, 11
Clive Spong (Linden Artists): Front and Back Covers

Editorial Assistance
Proofreading by Joanna Chapman; indexing by David Squire

PRINTED IN BELGIUM BY

INTERNATIONAL BOOK PRODUCTION